FENG SHUI
STEP BY STEP

FENG SHUI
STEP BY STEP

Arranging Your Home for Health and Happiness—
with Personalized Astrological Charts

T. RAPHAEL SIMONS

CROWN TRADE PAPERBACKS
NEW YORK

Text and illustrations copyright © 1996 by T. Raphael Simons

Published by Crown Trade Paperbacks, 201 East 50th Street, New York, New York 10022. Member of the Crown Publishing Group.

Random House, Inc. New York, Toronto, London, Sydney, Auckland
http://www.randomhouse.com/

Printed in the United States of America

Design by Susan DeStaebler

Library of Congress Cataloging-in-Publication Data is available upon request.

ISBN 0-517-88794-0

10   9   8   7   6   5   4

Dedicated to the memory of
Leon and Netty Simons

ACKNOWLEDGMENTS

To Tao Chun, who first brought me to this work, I owe a special debt of gratitude. I also wish to express my heartfelt thanks to Terry Lee, who taught me the authentic feng shui tradition; to the Reverend Yamamoto, who revealed the lucky star system to me; to all of my students, who taught me how to teach, and whose questions inspired the writing of this book; to Sue Herner, my agent, for her excellent guidance and sense of humor; to Carol Southern, my editor, whose remarkable insight and sense of form have helped me make the material of this book intelligible and coherent; to Ingrid Marcroft, my student and friend, who read the manuscript at the eleventh hour and came up with excellent suggestions to further clarify the text; and finally to you, dear reader, who, by implementing the material of this book, will be contributing positively to our much-needed raising of environmental consciousness.

CONTENTS

FENG SHUI
STEP BY STEP

How to Use This Book

On many occasions, people who have tried to use feng shui to arrange their homes have come to me, perplexed by what they have read on the subject, asking me to answer their questions and explain the techniques of feng shui in plain English.

Although feng shui is an elaborate art, it is not difficult to grasp when its rules and principles are systematically presented. The aim of this book is to set forth these principles and rules in a practical, step-by-step manner so that you will be able to use feng shui effectively and confidently to arrange your home.

You may have read or heard that there are three different schools of feng shui —the form school, the compass school, and the intuitive school. These are misnomers. There is only one authentic school of feng shui, which derives from the ancient Taoist tradition. It embraces a full range of techniques that include Chinese astrology, compass methods, form methods, and divining techniques.

Feng shui makes use of two Chinese astrological systems. These are called *ba tzu*, or "eight words," also called "the four pillars," and *jyo hsing*, or "nine stars," also called "the study of *chi*," and "the North Star method."

Ba tzu, which I use in my professional practice, is a sophisticated technique that is not practical for most Westerners, as it requires the ability to read and work with the Chinese lunar calendar and with a large number of Chinese characters. This book, instead, will make use of jyo hsing, or nine star astrology, an equally powerful technique that I also use in my practice.

Nine star is the oldest known horoscope system. It was originally set forth by Fu Hsi, the first king of China, in the fourth millennium B.C. Because of its straightforward, logical nature, I was able to organize the nine star material in the easy-to-use tables you will find in the following chapters. Nine star astrology is not to be underestimated. It is a fundamental system of Taoist science and is used by all true feng shui experts and knowledgeable laymen in China and Japan.

Relative to nine star astrology is an array of compass methods that I have worked out and arranged in tables. These compass methods will help you align such pieces of furniture as your bed, favorite chair, and desk so that you may enjoy better health, prosperity, and overall well-being. When you become familiar with these compass methods and put them to use—together with the guidelines I have provided for setting up the different rooms and areas of your home—you will experience the great benefit this profound art can bring.

I have also delineated the authentic feng shui system of colors for you to use. This system has three parts:

1. Your personal colors, as derived from your Chinese horoscope.

2. The use of colors to bring you and your space into harmony.

3. The use of colors to balance the energy of the space in itself, regardless of who lives in it.

The supplies you will need to put this book to use are: a few (Xerox) copies of the floor plan of your house or apartment, a pendulum, and a compass (which you can find in most hardware or sporting goods stores).

The floor plan doesn't have to be exact; however, it should be reasonably correct. If you don't have a copy of the architect's original plan, you can most easily draw your floor plan on graph paper. If you don't want to take the dimensions of your home and its rooms with a tape measure, simply pace out the length and breadth of your home and its rooms, estimating three feet in each step. Try to draw your floor plan on an 8½-by-11-inch sheet of paper for the sake of convenience.

A pendulum is essentially a weight that is suspended from a string or light chain. It can be of any shape and material as long as it swings and rotates freely.

You can easily make one out of a glass bead and string or thread. I personally prefer using a pendulum made of brass that is perfectly symmetrical. You can buy such a pendulum in most New Age book shops. A weight from a fishing line is also effective and is easily found in most sporting goods stores. A pendulum used for work indoors, where the air is calm, can be small and lightweight. Pendulums used outdoors, on the other hand, should be heavier. You will find complete instructions for use of the pendulum in chapter 25.

To read a compass correctly, stand facing squarely toward the direction you want to read. Hold your compass level in front of you. Turn the whole compass case in your hand until the north end of the needle points to the letter N on the azimuth ring. (The azimuth ring is the ring of degrees—north, east, south, and west—printed on the plate of your compass.) The north end of the needle is either coated with green phosphorous or marked "N." The earth's magnetic field causes this end of the needle to point toward the magnetic North Pole. To find your bearing, just read the direction and degree straight ahead of you on the azimuth ring of the compass.

As you proceed through the coming chapters you will be consulting Chinese astrological charts according to your birth date and listing the data that is specific for you. You will find the charts simple to use and you will find this data very effective in arranging your home harmoniously.

You may either list your personal data below or do so on a separate sheet of paper. If you live with others, draw vertical columns to create space for data for each person in your household. Then list the entries as indicated below.

PERSONAL DATA

1. Yin/Yang _____

   - Your physical makeup _____

   - Your occupation _____

   - Corresponding environmental needs _____

2. Your Chinese season of birth _____

   - Corresponding element _____

   - What it means for your personal environment _____

3. Your birth star number _____

   - Corresponding compass direction _____

   - The other directions in space that are in harmony with your birth star _____
   _____

   - Corresponding decorating guidelines (lines, patterns, shapes, colors) _____
   _____

4. The compass direction of your doorway _____

   - The harmony or discord of your birth star with your door's compass
   direction _____

   - The color to use to harmonize your birth star with your door's compass
   direction _____

5. Your mutually harmonious stars (for those who live together) _____

   - Their corresponding directions in space _____

   - Their corresponding decorating guidelines _____

6. Your lucky stars _____

   - Their corresponding directions in space _____

   - Their special corresponding colors _____

   - Their corresponding shapes and patterns _____

To enjoy the full benefit of this book, please read it chapter by chapter. Don't jump around. The material is developed step by step. Take your time to absorb the material. As you develop your understanding of feng shui, you will be able to work with it in a more and more creative and personally meaningful way.

It is my wish that you will become able to use the wonderful art of feng shui so that it effectively transforms your environment, supports your health, and clears the way to realizing your goals in life.

part one

UNDERSTANDING CHI

HEAVEN, EARTH, AND MAN

Alignment and balance are the core and essence of feng shui. They have both internal and external significance for practitioners.

It is said that in very ancient times, feng shui was only practiced inwardly, and that wherever its practitioner went, the world was filled with joy and contentment. But in the past several thousand years, as life has become more and more complicated and the world has fallen into discord and strife, it has been necessary for feng shui to be practiced outwardly as well.

Feng shui has two premises and two levels of practice. The first premise is that man's state of mind and energy affects his environment for good or ill. The second premise is that the condition of the environment affects man's internal state.

In practice, the inner level involves concentration techniques such as contemplation of the principles of the *I Ching* (or *The Book of Changes*), meditation, and *chi kung* (a system of internal exercises to promote good health and healing). The outer level consists of horoscope, compass, form, and divining techniques.

The inner and outer levels are like two sides of a coin. They are inseparable and interdependent. To illustrate more fully, let's look at an image called the "three coordinate powers." The three coordinate powers are heaven, earth, and man. Heaven corresponds to time. Earth corresponds to space.

The human relationship to heaven and to earth constitutes the outer level. Horoscopes are drawn to find your relationship to heaven. Compass and form methods, based on the same underlying principles as horoscope methods, are used to find and adjust your relationship to earth.

To understand how the principles of heaven and earth relate to one another—how they balance and interact with one another, and how they can be brought together in perfect harmony in man—constitutes the inner level.

The principles of heaven and earth are the father and mother of all phenomena. Man uses the principles of heaven and earth for good or ill. When we live in harmony with our essential nature and allow the principles of heaven and earth to interact freely and naturally through us, our environment becomes harmonious and radiant with vital energy. Conversely, if we lose the real character of our essential nature and abuse the principles of heaven and earth, our environment falls into confusion and discord. To quote Chuang Tzu, "If you get the Tao, there is no effect that cannot be produced; if you miss it, there is no effect that can."

EXERCISE

This is one of the first exercises I learned in feng shui. It is an excellent method for simultaneously applying inner and outer approaches and becoming aware of the space around you. Let it become second nature to you.

To begin, you may either sit or stand in the space. Let your posture be balanced and relaxed. Breathe naturally and calmly. Concentrate, and gently let go of your thoughts. Just be in the space without any preconceptions about it. Next, simply walk about the space for a while. Become aware of your intuitive responses and impressions. Where is there more energy? Where is there less energy? Where is the energy powerful? Where is it depleted? Where is it positive? Where is it negative? Try this in different spaces. After a while you will get the knack of it.

CHI

Chi is sometimes described as the cosmic breath, or as the vital principle. It is the essence of the principles of heaven and earth, of time and space, and therefore of all relative phenomena; it is the force of change and transformation.

Chi is displayed in the circling of the heavens, the seasons and weather patterns, the undulations of the land and the tides of the sea, the changes in our bodies, emotions, and thoughts, and the changes of our affairs and fortunes. Everything breathes and moves in accord with it. Everything comes from it, exists through it, and returns to it.

The cycle of chi, of arising and vanishing, is common to everything, even to solid rock. Although it appears unchanging to man, over the life span of the universe, it appears and disappears in a flash. Or, as Chuang Tzu nicely put it, "A frog in a well cannot be talked with about the sea; he is confined to the limits of his space. An insect of summer cannot be talked with about ice; it knows nothing beyond its own time."

As chi is the cosmic breath, the cosmos, or universe, is that which breathes. The cosmos is understood in Taoist science as an organic being that is full of life, depicted sometimes as a great dragon coursing through time, space, heaven, and earth.

The dragon symbolizes the spirit of fertility and nourishment. As such, it emerges from the depths of the ocean and soars into the sky. It appears in storm clouds and lightning. Its voice is the thunder. It plummets to the earth in rain, and rises in abundant crops. As the imperial symbol of ancient China, it also represents creativity, wealth, and wisdom.

Feng shui experts, called dragon people, or *lung jen* in Chinese, view the environment as an expression of chi. They understand the principles of its generation and destruction, and they know the secrets of its transformation.

Chi has three phases. They are called sheng, si, and sha. *Sheng* means moving upward, or waxing; *si* means dying, or waning; and *sha* indicates harmful energy.

SHENG CHI

A place has sheng chi when it feels fresh and bright, the animals are healthy, the people are prosperous and happy, and when it overlooks a beautiful park, a garden, the woods, mountains, a field, a river, a lake, or the ocean. You have sheng chi when you feel positive aspiration. The moon approaching full is sheng.

SI CHI

A place has si chi if it is dilapidated and unkempt, if the earth is depleted and the vegetation is poor, the animals are sick, and the people are weak and impoverished. You have si chi when you are depressed. The moon approaching new is si.

SHA CHI

You have sha chi when you are extremely angry. A place has sha chi when it feels strange or dangerous. Sha comes from negative conditions both below and aboveground. Sha below ground is sometimes called "noxious rays"; aboveground it is sometimes called "secret arrows."

Noxious rays drain energy and cause illness. In a place where this condition exists you might become fatigued and nervous for no apparent reason. A house that is built on low stagnant ground, around which the air hangs heavy, is one example of this sort of place. A house that stands above an underground cave is another. (You will find more examples, as well as cures for this condition, in chapter 25).

Secret arrows are irritating conditions that originate aboveground. They attack the nerves and contribute to such misfortunes as illness, disrupted relationships, and professional and financial troubles. Secret arrows come against a house if a road or water runs directly toward or away from any of its doors or windows (fig. 1); if it stands at the end of a T-junction (fig. 2); if it stands at the end of a blind alley or is positioned so that a corner of another building points directly at its door or windows (fig. 3); if the front door partly faces the edge of another building and partly faces an empty lot (fig. 4). Other examples of secret arrows are if sharp objects point at the door or windows; if the front door is directly in line with a flagpole or lamppost; if the door or windows directly face a steeply pointed roof; if there is a building across the way that is falling into ruin; if there is a dead or dying tree directly in front of the door or windows; if railroad tracks or hanging electrical wires run glaringly across the view from the door or windows; if the house is completely hemmed in, or overwhelmed by being close to such structures as freeways, huge bridges, buildings that tower above it, or tower antennas; if a police or fire station, an armory, a casino, or other place of unusually disturbing activity, or a hospital, funeral home, or graveyard is visible from the door or windows; if glaring lights or blinking neon signs are visible from the windows; and if there are disruptive social conditions in the neighborhood such as loud noise and violence.

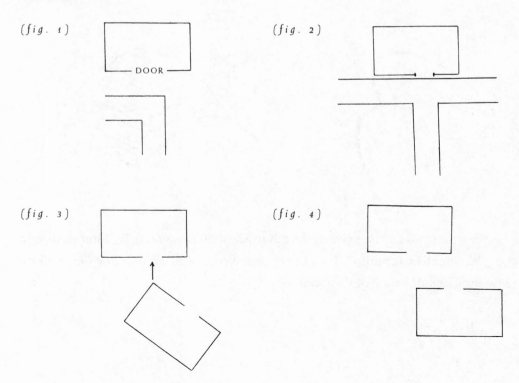

(fig. 1)

DOOR

(fig. 2)

(fig. 3)

(fig. 4)

A rugged-appearing mountain that rises abruptly (fig. 5); a mountain that is shaped like a terrace (fig. 6); a mountain that is unusually round, or one in the shape called the "breaker of luck" (fig. 7) or the "eye of a horse" (fig. 8) also sends out secret arrows. The more the mountain dominates the view, the stronger its effect. A mountain seen on the distant horizon has far less of an effect than one that is close up.

(fig. 5) *(fig. 6)*

(fig. 7) *(fig. 8)*

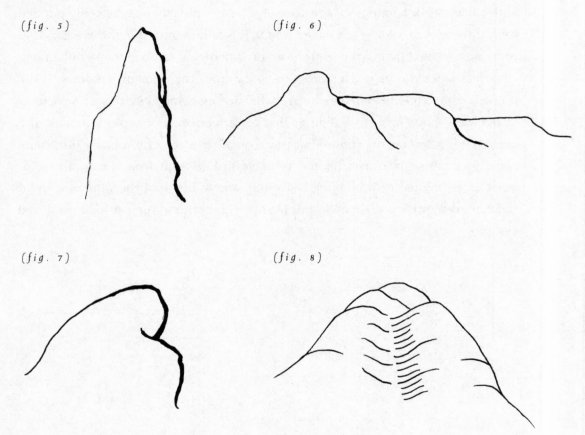

Secret arrows can be produced from inside a house as well, by interior design and placement of furniture. This condition, along with all its remedies, will be fully discussed in Part 2 of this book.

EXERCISES

1. Note the quality of the chi in your house and in the houses of others. Is it sheng or si? Look carefully out the front and back doors and windows. Do you detect any visible sources of sha?

2. When out walking, take note of the conditions of chi. Develop your perception by observing the plant life, animals, and people. Does the environment have sheng, si, or sha chi? Can you find different qualities of chi in environmental details that are close together? When practicing feng shui, it is always important to take into account the conditions of chi surrounding your house.

3. Try to sense the quality of chi coming from below ground. Relax. Breathe calmly and clear your mind. Allow your mind's eye to open. Notice how you feel. Do you receive any impressions? What are they? What do they tell you? Is the chi sheng, si, or sha? You don't have to be standing on the ground to feel its chi. High-rise buildings act like amplifiers: the chi from below ground will become more and more magnified the higher up you go. (In chapter 25, I will discuss in detail various methods for divining underground chi.)

YIN AND YANG

Yin and *yang* are the negative and positive phases in the cyclic flow of chi. They are the root of power, the beginning of everything, and, as they constitute the basic principles of the entire universe, they are the cause of life and death. The Chinese say that the sky is yang and the earth is yin. Yang is active and yin is restful, and, as activity culminates in rest and rest culminates in activity, yang becomes yin and yin becomes yang. What originates with yang is received and completed by yin. They are inseparable; the one implies the other. Or, as Lao-tzu put it:

> *So it is that existence and nonexistence give birth the one to the idea of the other; that difficulty and ease produce in the one the idea of the other; that length and shortness fashion out of the one the figure of the other; that the ideas of height and depth arise from the contrast of the one with the other; that the musical notes and tones become harmonious through the relation of one with another; and that being before and behind give the idea of one following another.*

Yin and yang are aspects of chi that relate to your physical makeup, your occupation, and your home. Yang contracts and produces density, gravity, heat, and activity. Yin expands and produces diffusion, lightness, cold, and quiescence. The yang personality is active, commanding, concentrated, fiery; the yin personality is more inclusive, diffuse, gentle, tranquil, magnetic.

Yang	Yin
outdoors	indoors
high	low
bright	dark
hot	cold
fire	water
day	night
spring – summer	fall – winter
mountain	valley
street corner	middle of the block
time	space

YOUR PHYSICAL MAKEUP

Since the day you were born, your physical makeup has been either yin or yang. To tell which it is, look at your face in the mirror while referring to the two descriptions below. You will probably find characteristics of both types reflected in your features. If you are uncertain which predominates, look at your eyes. If they are close or deep set, you are yang—if they are far apart or tend to bulge, you are yin.

THE YANG TYPE

Imagine a line running down the middle of your face from your forehead to your chin. In the yang type, the features of the face are concentrated toward this middle line. The eyes are close together, deep set, and narrow; the eyebrows are slanted toward the bridge of the nose; the nose is more or less small, possibly flat; the cheekbones are strong and pronounced, and the lower jaw is large and square; the mouth is rather small and the lips are thin; and the lines in the face appear to be more vertical than horizontal. The yang type originates under harsh conditions, such as are found in the extreme latitudes of the earth, extreme climates, and mountainous regions—very cold (yin) environments.

THE YIN TYPE

In the yin type the facial features diverge from the middle line. There may be a cleft running down the center of the face, producing two distinct lobes in the forehead, a cleft at the tip of the nose, parted front teeth, and a cleft chin; the eyes are wide, far apart, and may even protrude; the eyebrows slant away from the center of the face; the nose is long, or large, and protrudes; the cheekbones are slight, and the lower jaw is slanted from the chin up to the ears; the mouth is large and the lips are full; and the lines in the face appear to be more horizontal than vertical. The yin type originates under mild conditions, such as are found in tropical latitudes, temperate climates, and oceanic areas.

YIN AND YANG OCCUPATIONS

If you are constitutionally yin, you naturally express yourself more through thoughts. If you are constitutionally yang, you naturally express yourself more through actions. Over and above that, however, it is possible, if you are constitutionally yin, to cultivate a yang occupation, and if you are constitutionally yang, to cultivate a yin occupation.

Yin occupations include research, scholarship, teaching, writing, and all other activities that require more mental exertion. Yang occupations include business, sales, travel, sports, performing arts, engineering, mechanics, armed services, police, and all other indoor and outdoor activities that require more physical exertion.

YOUR MOST SUITABLE ENVIRONMENT

You need to consider two things when choosing your proper environment: the first is what is appropriate for your physical makeup, and the second is what is appropriate for your type of occupation. In the case of your physical makeup, you need to choose an environment that complements you. In other words, you need your opposite. For example, if your physical makeup is yang, your space should be generally yin, and if your physical makeup is yin, your space should be generally yang.

In the case of your occupation, you need to choose an environment that conforms to your occupation. For example, if your occupation is yang, you should have an area in your space that is yang to stimulate your activity. If your occupation is yin, you should have an area that is yin to bring about deep thinking.

In summing up:

1. If your physical makeup is yang and your occupation is yang, your space should be predominantly yin with a special yang area.

2. If your physical makeup is yang and your occupation is yin, your space should be, for the most part, yin.

3. If your physical makeup is yin and your occupation is yin, your space should be predominantly yang with a special yin area.

4. If your physical makeup is yin and your occupation is yang, your space should be, for the most part, yang.

A yang environment has warm, active colors and lighting; a yin environment has cool, restful colors and lighting. A yang environment is very stimulating; it could be high up or on a street corner. A yin environment is calming; and could be low down or in the middle of the block.

The above information should serve as one of your basic guidelines for arranging your home. In the second part of this book you will see how this information about yin and yang can be developed and modified to suit the particular needs of each room, or area, in your home.

EXERCISES

1. Study your face while keeping in mind the descriptions of the yin and yang types. Which type are you? What does it tell you about your environmental needs?

2. Is your occupation yin or yang? What does it say about the environmental needs of your work?

3. Write down what you find out in your list of personal data.

4. If you live with someone else, write down his/her data in your list as well.

chapter 4

THE FIVE ELEMENTS

In addition to the three phases, sheng, si, and sha, and the two aspects, yin and yang, chi has five moods, or elements. The five elements are called Water, Wood, Fire, Earth, and Metal. The elements operate in the lives of all people at all times, but, as everyone is unique, one of the elements will be more pronounced in the personality of one person than another.

The descriptions of these elements with their correspondences, as set forth in this chapter, will introduce you to a very important conceptual tool. With it you will be able to better understand your environment and its subtle connections to your health and career. It is the key to the scientific transformation of the chi of your environment. As you proceed through this book, you will learn more and more about how to apply it.

The elements are characterized by natural settings, and have a large number of correspondences, or attributes. For convenience, I will simply list the attributes of each element in turn. When you come to the section corresponding to your season of birth, enter it, its corresponding element, and what it means for your personal environment on your personal data sheet.

WATER

Water flows. It moves along the line of least resistance to find its way to the ocean, where it comes and goes in tides and waves. It is a carrier. It cleanses, refreshes, and restores all life. We travel over and through it. Places where water abounds, such as near oceans, rivers, lakes, wetlands, and cities with canals, such as Amsterdam and Venice, come under the sway of Water.

YOUR SEASON OF BIRTH

The season associated with Water is winter, which, according to the Chinese calendar, is from November 7th to February 4th. If you were born in the season of Water, there is a deeply emotional aspect to your personality. You may be outgoing; however, you may also keep your deepest feelings quite hidden. Your home environment, therefore, should provide you with a place for privacy and solitude.

MENTAL AND PHYSICAL STATES

The positive mental states of Water are wisdom, intelligence, reflection, willpower, and ambition. Its negative states are fear, trembling, and coldness.

The internal organs and parts of the body associated with Water are the kidneys, the adrenals, the bladder, the sexual organs, the blood and the lymph system, the bones, the bone marrow, the teeth, the nerves, the brain, and the ears.

Imbalances of Water are associated with such physical and emotional conditions as kidney diseases, digestive problems, edema, bloating, blood poisoning, low metabolism, high or low blood pressure, hypertension, sexual debility, infertility, swollen joints, rheumatism, arthritis, tooth decay, phobias, nervousness, blocking of the emotions and thoughts, depression, and lethargy.

You will find complete instructions on how to balance the elements of your space so that it supports your well-being and encourages healing in the coming chapters, especially in the second part of this book.

OCCUPATIONS

Occupations corresponding to Water involve research, investigation, and diplomacy and include commerce, transportation, businesses dealing with foods, teas, coffee, liquors, drugs and pharmaceuticals, hypnotherapy, psychotherapy, massage therapy, hydrotherapy, and all occupations in which water is used. On the negative side, as Water runs underground, it corresponds to the activities of organized crime.

SHAPES AND COLORS

The basic shape of Water is wave-like. Its land formations are those which undulate (fig. 9), its building shapes are labyrinthine, curved, and asymmetrical. The stylistic themes of Water for interior decor consist of smooth and flowing forms and patterns. The colors of Water are black and navy.

(fig. 9)

WEATHER, FLOWER, AND DIRECTIONS IN SPACE

The weather corresponding to Water is cold. The flower traditionally assigned to winter, the season of Water, is the plum blossom, which symbolizes long life.

The direction in space for Water is north.

PARTS OF THE HOME

In the home, Water corresponds to the plumbing, as well as to the bath, the study, and the meditation room.

A house with defective plumbing or other problems pointing to Water, such as clutter or disrepair in the north section, may negatively affect corresponding areas of your emotional and physical well-being and hinder the smooth flow of your professional and financial affairs.

WOOD

Wood springs. It is strong and flexible. It bends under the force of the wind and adapts to the changes of the seasons. Its roots go deep. It spreads forth its leaves, bears sweet flowers and fruits, and produces seeds for the future. All woodlands and rain forests, and cities with towering skyscrapers are ruled by it.

Your Season of Birth

The season associated with Wood is spring, which according to the Chinese calendar is from February 4th to May 5th. If you were born in the season of Wood you are forever optimistic and youthful. You are irrepressible and full of ideas, and you succeed by single-mindedness. Your home should have a special place for your books, music, and works of art, and a place where you can concentrate, study, and create.

Mental and Physical States

The positive mental states associated with Wood are kindness, friendliness, generosity, romantic love, the ability to plan and decide, and the capacity for coordination and control. Its negative state is anger.

The internal organs and parts of the body associated with Wood are the liver, the gallbladder, the muscles, the sinews, the tendons, the ligaments, the nails, the hands, the feet, and the eyes.

Imbalances of Wood are associated with such physical and emotional conditions as liver and gallbladder disorders, poor eyesight, back pains, weakness of the limbs, cramping, paralysis, shock, irritability, confusion, repressed emotions and thoughts, fears of being trapped, and inability to make plans and decisions.

Occupations

Occupations associated with Wood involve planning and include architectural and landscape designing, interior decorating, fashion designing, musical composition, teaching, writing, painting, photography, lighting, and cinematography.

Shapes and Colors

The basic shape associated with Wood is rectangular and upright. Its corresponding land formations extend up and down rather steeply (fig. 10); buildings that correspond to it are tall, relatively narrow, and have flat roofs, and its stylistic themes for interior decor consist of rectangular forms and pattern motifs. The colors of Wood are all the greens and blues except for navy and midnight blue, which correspond to Water.

(fig. 10)

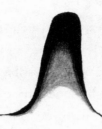

WEATHER, FLOWER, AND DIRECTIONS IN SPACE

The weather associated with Wood is rain. The flower traditionally associated with springtime, the season of Wood, is the peony, which symbolizes love.

The directions in space for Wood are east and southeast.

PARTS OF THE HOME

In the home, Wood corresponds to the structural framework, as well as to the living room, the music room, the "entertainment unit," the art studio, the library, and the study.

A house with a weak, damaged, or poorly designed structural framework, or other problems pointing to Wood, such as clutter or disrepair in the east or southeast sections, may negatively affect corresponding areas of your physical and emotional well-being and inhibit your ability to make timely plans and decisions.

FIRE

Fire shines. It is hot, dry, and cheerful. It is alive and spirited. Red, jagged mountains, such as those in Arizona, and burning hot deserts are under its rulership.

YOUR SEASON OF BIRTH

The season associated with Fire is summer, which according to the Chinese calendar is from May 5th to August 7th. If you were born in the season of Fire, there is a fiery aspect to your personality. You love to rise and shine in life. Love itself is vital to your happiness. You may also be artistically inclined. Your home should be a place of beauty and warmth, not necessarily a place in which to entertain all the time, as you also love your privacy, but a place that delights the senses.

MENTAL AND PHYSICAL STATES

The positive mental states of Fire are courtesy, courage, zeal, joy, and love. Its negative states are hyperactivity, confusion, impulsiveness, and rashness.

The internal organs and parts of the body associated with Fire are the heart, small intestine, the tongue, the "triple heater"—the regulator of the digestive fire and the warmth of the upper, middle, and lower regions of the torso—and the function called "heart constrictor," which maintains feelings of love, protects the heart, and controls the immune function.

Imbalances of Fire are associated with such physical and emotional conditions as fever, heart disease, high blood pressure, poor circulation, coldness of the extremities, numbness, neuromuscular tensions, digestive problems, malnutrition due to poor assimilation of food, problems with eyesight, speech impediments, emotional upsets and confusions, sexual excess or coldness, joylessness, and broken-heartedness.

OCCUPATIONS

Occupations corresponding to Fire include the fine arts, garden designing, the medical arts, teaching, inventing, mathematics, electronics, computers, accounting, cooking, and all occupations that involve the use of fire.

SHAPES AND COLORS

The basic shape of Fire is triangular. Its land formations are sharp, jagged, and pointed (fig. 11). Buildings associated with it have pointed roofs or spires, and stylistic themes for interior decor consist of radiant patterns and cheerful displays of flowers and works of art. The colors of Fire range from dark purples to bright reds. Purple is sometimes called the "heart of fire."

(fig. 11)

WEATHER, FLOWER, AND DIRECTIONS IN SPACE

The weather associated with Fire is hot. The flower traditionally associated with summer, the season of Fire, is the lotus, which symbolizes fruitfulness.

The direction in space for Fire is south.

PARTS OF THE HOME

In the home, Fire is related to the heating system, the hearth, and the stove, as well as to the kitchen, the living room, the porch, the patio, and the gardens.

A house with a poor or defective heating system or stove, or other problems pointing to Fire, such as clutter or disrepair in the south section, may negatively affect corresponding areas of your physical and emotional well-being, and inhibit your productivity at work.

EARTH

Earth supports. It is the container of all the other elements. It is central. It is the ground that bears up life and nourishment. It transmutes dead organisms to new forms of life. It is the great cauldron of life. It is solid and receptive, fertile, full, deep, broad, and balanced. The Great Plains, which are rich with wheat and corn, are ruled by it. It embodies the golden mean and the state of equanimity by which the golden mean is realized. When we practice equanimity our world becomes balanced and full of life. When, on the other hand, we become one-sided and petty, our world deteriorates. Or as Confucius, in *The Doctrine of the Mean*, puts it:

> *While there are no stirrings of pleasure, anger, sorrow, or joy, the mind may be said to be in the state of equilibrium. When those feelings have been stirred, and they act in their due degree, there ensues what may be called the state of harmony. This equilibrium is the great root from which grow all the human actings in the world, and this harmony is the universal path which they all should pursue. Let the states of equilibrium and harmony exist in perfection, and a happy order will prevail throughout heaven and earth, and all things will be nourished and flourish.*

Your Season of Birth

There is no season assigned to Earth. All seasons belong to it. However, Earth is said to become strongest at the end of the summer, which, according to the Chinese calendar, is from the end of July to August 7th. If you were born at the end of the Fire season, when Earth is most productive, you have the capacity to be supportive of others. You are productive, trustworthy, and gentle. Your home, besides being beautiful and warm, should be especially comfortable. It should have a very workable kitchen, a comfortable dining room, and a special workroom or work area.

Mental and Physical States

The positive mental states associated with Earth, beside equanimity, are truthfulness, trustworthiness, patience, sympathy, compassion, firmness, and determination. Its negative state is worry.

The internal organs and parts of the body associated with Earth are the stomach, the pancreas, the spleen, the flesh, and the mouth.

Physical and emotional disorders associated with unbalanced Earth include diseases of the stomach, pancreas, and spleen, eating disorders, digestive problems, obesity, malnutrition, diabetes, abdominal swelling, wasting away of the flesh, infertility, insomnia, nervousness, anxiety, confusion, insecurity, craving for attention, greed, and loneliness.

Occupations

Occupations that correspond to Earth involve all forms of service, including construction, building, real estate, the food industry, marketing, banking, investing and brokerage, the health care industry, and all charities.

Shapes and Colors

The basic shape of Earth is square. Its land formations are broad and flat (fig. 12), its building shapes are broad and square, and its stylistic themes for interior decor consist of broad, flat surfaces and square forms and pattern motifs. The colors corresponding to Earth range from browns through oranges to yellows.

(*fig. 12*)

WEATHER, FLOWER, AND DIRECTIONS IN SPACE

The weather associated with Earth is cloudy and/or windy. As the earth is strongest at the end of summer, its flower is the lotus, the symbol of fruitfulness.

The directions in space for Earth are the middle, the southwest, and the northeast.

PARTS OF THE HOME

In the home, Earth corresponds to the floor, the walls, and the masonry, as well as to the kitchen, the pantry, the dining room, the workroom, and the basement.

A house with cracked or crumbling floors, walls, or masonry, or other problems pointing to Earth, such as clutter or disrepair in the middle, the southwest or northeast sections may negatively affect corresponding areas of your physical and emotional well-being, and undermine the growth of your professional affairs.

METAL

Metal reinforces. It is the perfection of Earth. It is also the great expanse of the sky that arches like a dome. It runs through the earth in veins. It is malleable and versatile, and is used to make such things as coins, bells, cutlery, mirrors, jewelry, pots and pans, machines, vehicles, construction equipment, wires, communication devices, computers, and so on.

YOUR SEASON OF BIRTH

The season associated with Metal is autumn, the harvest season, which according to the Chinese calendar is from August 7th to November 7th. If you were born in the Metal season, you may be something of a perfectionist. You have a strong force of personality. You have the ability to use experience to gain wisdom. You may have interests in education, research, and the spiritual sciences. Your home should be neat and orderly, with an interesting library and a quiet study—a place where you can think deeply.

MENTAL AND PHYSICAL STATES

The positive mental states of Metal are sternness, morality, justice, and the sense of rhythmical order. Its negative states are grief and inflexibility.

The internal organs and parts of the body corresponding to Metal are the lungs, the large intestine, the skin, and the nose.

Imbalances of Metal are associated with such physical and mental conditions as diseases of the lungs and large intestine, skin problems, degeneration of the spinal vertebrae, emotional blockages, melancholy, and hypochondria.

OCCUPATIONS

Occupations corresponding to Metal involve order and refinement. They include law, the police, the military, telecommunications, computers, the arts, perfume manufacturing, metallurgy, mechanical and electronic engineering, and so on.

SHAPES AND COLORS

The basic shapes of Metal are round and oval. You can see them in land formations that are well rounded (fig. 13) and in such constructions as domes and cupolas. Stylistic themes for interior decor consist of smooth and rounded forms and patterns. The colors of Metal range from gray through silver to white.

(*fig. 13*)

WEATHER, FLOWER, AND DIRECTIONS IN SPACE

The weather associated with Metal is clear and fine, like mountain air. The flower traditionally associated with autumn, the season of Metal, is the chrysanthemum, which symbolizes joy.

The directions in space for Metal are west and northwest.

PARTS OF THE HOME

In the home, Metal corresponds to the electrical and telephone wiring, as well as to the locks and other security devices. It also corresponds to the study and library.

A house with defective electrical or telephone wiring, or without proper security, or with other problems pointing to Metal, such as clutter or disrepair in the west or northwest sections, may negatively affect corresponding areas of your physical and emotional well-being, and interrupt the rhythmic order of your professional affairs.

THE THREE CYCLES

Now that we have looked at the five elements separately, let's look at them together to see how they interact with one another.

The five elements relate to one another according to three basic cycles: the cycle of generation, the cycle of destruction, and the cycle of mitigation. Let's first look at the cycles of generation and destruction.

THE CYCLE OF GENERATION	THE CYCLE OF DESTRUCTION
Water feeds Wood	Water puts out Fire
Wood feeds Fire	Fire melts Metal
Fire generates Earth	Metal cuts Wood
Earth creates Metal	Wood breaks up Earth
Metal holds Water	Earth absorbs Water

The interrelationships of these cycles can be seen in figure 14:

(*fig. 14*)

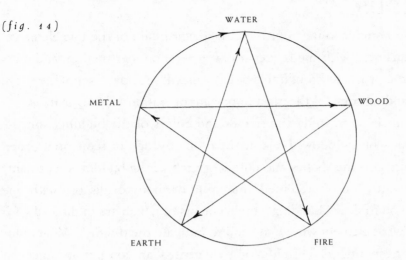

The elements going clockwise around the circle are in the order of generation, and in the star formation, according to the arrows, are in the order of destruction. Note how the order of destruction comes about by always skipping over one element. Note also how the skipped element serves to mitigate the conflict of the two on either side of it. Thus we have the third cycle:

THE CYCLE OF MITIGATION

Water mitigates the conflict of Metal with Wood
Wood mitigates the conflict of Water with Fire
Fire mitigates the conflict of Wood with Earth
Earth mitigates the conflict of Fire with Metal
Metal mitigates the conflict of Earth with Water

Here is a brief example of how the cycle of mitigation can be used: If you were born in a year of the element Wood—1952—and the door of your home faces the direction of the element Metal, or West, you would decorate the area around the doorway with the color of the element Water—or midnight blue—to create harmony. This operation and others similar to it will be fully illustrated in the coming chapters.

EXERCISES

1. Copy and/or commit to memory the circled star figure of the five elements. Become acquainted with the sequences of generation, destruction, and mitigation. As you proceed through this book, you will see how essential they are for understanding some of the most important operations of feng shui.

2. If you live in the city, study the shapes and colors of the buildings on the street outside your window. Look at them one by one in sequential order. What elements do the shapes and colors of each of the buildings represent? Do the elements, thus represented, line up in harmony or discord with one another? If you find two buildings, the elements of which are in discord with each other, what element would you add to mitigate the discord? What color or shape corresponds to the mitigating element? Can you put an object of that color and/or shape in the window to interact harmoniously with the discordant elements outside? For example, if outside your window you see a building that is red (corresponding to Fire) next to one that is white (corresponding to Metal), you could put something yellow (corresponding to Earth)—yellow flowers, yellow curtains, a yellow stone, or an object made of yellow glass—at the window to mitigate the discord.

3. If you live in the country, look out the doors and windows of your house. Study the terrain. Note the shapes and colors of the different land formations. What elements do they represent? If they seem to be in discordant relationships with one another, what element might you add to mitigate the discord? What color or shape corresponds to the mitigating element? Can you put something of that color or shape by your doorway or in your window to balance the discordant elements outside?

4. If you have not yet done so, list your Chinese season of birth, its corresponding element, and what that means for your home environment on your sheet of personal data. For example, if you were born in June, you were born in the Chinese summer, or the season of Fire. This means that your home should be a place of beauty and warmth, a delightful place where you can entertain as well as have privacy. If you live with someone else, write down his/her season of birth, its element, and what that means for your home as well.

THE NINE STARS

So far, you have seen how your yin and yang physical constitution and occupation, as well as the element (Water, Wood, Fire, Earth, Metal) of the season in which you were born, affect your personality and environmental requirements. Let's look now at the nine star astrological system, which provides more refined horoscope information than the five elements. We will examine how the nine stars work through both time and space to determine your personality and the chi of your home, and how you can bring these two factors together in perfect harmony.

THE MAP OF THE ELEMENTS

The directions in space assigned to the elements are north for Water; east and southeast for Wood; south for Fire; southwest, northeast, and the middle for Earth; and west and northwest for Metal. If we make a map of them they look like figure 15 on the following page.

These nine spatial directions are analogues of the nine stars. Each star is assigned a number, a yin or yang aspect, an element, and a compass direction, as you can see in the table following figure 15.

(*fig. 15*)

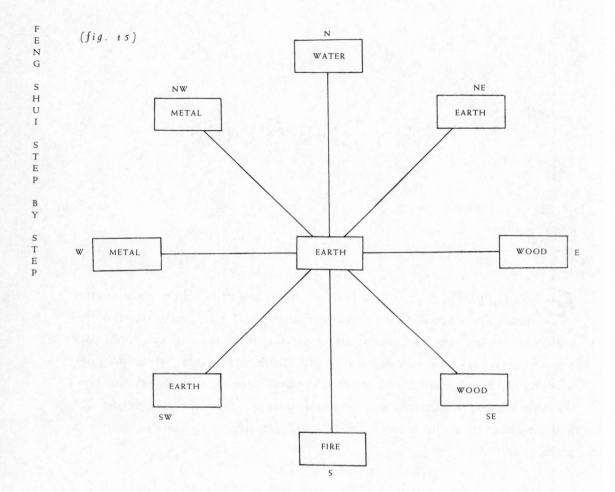

Star Number	Yin/Yang	Element	Compass Direction
1	Yin	Water	North
2	Yin	Earth	Southwest
3	Yang	Wood	East
4	Yin	Wood	Southeast
5	Yin/Yang	Earth	Middle
6	Yang	Metal	Northwest
7	Yin	Metal	West
8	Yang	Earth	Northeast
9	Yang	Fire	South

The stars are called 1 Water Star, 2 Earth Star, 3 Wood Star, and so forth.

According to your date of birth, you came into this life under one or another of these stars, or moods of chi. The chi of the year of your birth is therefore the chi of your basic character, and, expressed as a star/element, is that which determines the favorable directions in space for you.

You will find your birth star in the tables below. Please note that males and females born in the same year have different stars. This is because Taoist science, in viewing the male and female as mirrors of each other, requires that their horoscopes be calculated in opposite ways. Note also that the Chinese solar year, used in the nine star calculation, begins on February 4th (or 15 degrees Aquarius). If your date of birth falls before February 4th, look to the prior year to find your birth star. For example, if your date of birth was February 3, 1960, your birth star is that of 1959. Enter your birth star, its corresponding direction in space, the other directions in space that are in harmony with it, and its corresponding decorating guidelines on your personal data list.

Year of Birth	Male Star	Female Star
1915	4	2
1916	3	3
1917	2	4
1918	1	5
1919	9	6
1920	8	7
1921	7	8
1922	6	9
1923	5	1
1924	4	2
1925	3	3
1926	2	4
1927	1	5
1928	9	6
1929	8	7
1930	7	8

Year of Birth	Male Star	Female Star
1931	6	9
1932	5	1
1933	4	2
1934	3	3
1935	2	4
1936	1	5
1937	9	6
1938	8	7
1939	7	8
1940	6	9
1941	5	1
1942	4	2
1943	3	3
1944	2	4
1945	1	5
1946	9	6
1947	8	7
1948	7	8
1949	6	9
1950	5	1
1951	4	2
1952	3	3
1953	2	4
1954	1	5
1955	9	6
1956	8	7
1957	7	8
1958	6	9
1959	5	1
1960	4	2
1961	3	3
1962	2	4
1963	1	5
1964	9	6

Year of Birth	Male Star	Female Star
1965	8	7
1966	7	8
1967	6	9
1968	5	1
1969	4	2
1970	3	3
1971	2	4
1972	1	5
1973	9	6
1974	8	7
1975	7	8
1976	6	9
1977	5	1
1978	4	2
1979	3	3
1980	2	4
1981	1	5
1982	9	6
1983	8	7
1984	7	8
1985	6	9
1986	5	1
1987	4	2
1988	3	3
1989	2	4
1990	1	5
1991	9	6
1992	8	7
1993	7	8
1994	6	9
1995	5	1
1996	4	2
1997	3	3
1998	2	4

YEAR OF BIRTH	MALE STAR	FEMALE STAR
1999	1	5
2000	9	6
2001	8	7
2002	7	8
2003	6	9
2004	5	1
2005	4	2
2006	3	3
2007	2	4
2008	1	5
2009	9	6
2010	8	7
2011	7	8
2012	6	9
2013	5	1
2014	4	2
2015	3	3

Each of the nine stars exhibits a distinct personality as listed below. They are grouped according to the elements in the order: 1 Water Star; 3 and 4 Wood Stars; 9 Fire Star; 2, 5, and 8 Earth Stars; and 6 and 7 Metal Stars. Where there are two or three stars under one element, a basic personality description of the element precedes the personality descriptions of its related stars.

Included with the description of each of the nine star types is a list of favorable directions in space that you will use when deciding upon the alignment of such articles of furniture as your bed. The complete technique of alignment, however, will be discussed in the second part of this book. Please wait until you have read Part 2 to begin moving your furniture around.

1 Water Star

It is natural for you to be secretive while appearing to be outgoing. You have the knack of reading minds and acting covertly. Although you are usually quiet and reflective, you act forcefully to get your way. You can be stubborn and opinionated, and by refusing to listen, endanger your relationships. Your capacity for love is deep nonetheless, and your sexual energy is intense. You need a mate who positively responds to your passions while understanding your need for privacy and solitude.

You can become fearful and fretful if you don't have the space and time you need for meditation. If you cultivate it, however, your natural wisdom readily shines forth to the great benefit of all whom you love, and all you love to do.

OCCUPATIONS

You are better suited for occupations that require mental rather than physical exertion, such as writing, psychology, scientific and financial research, detective work, and pharmacology. You can also do well in sales, police work, nursing, the restaurant and bar business, and any occupation that involves liquids. You also have the capacity to undertake menial work cheerfully, especially if it is done as a form of spiritual service.

COMPATIBILITY

You are most compatible with 3 Wood Star, 4 Wood Star, 6 Metal Star, 7 Metal Star, and 9 Fire Star, moderately compatible with 1 Water Star, and least compatible with 2 Earth Star, 5 Earth Star, and 8 Earth Star.

HEALTH

You should be careful not to allow your body to become weak. You can become addicted to medicine. You are very sensitive to cold and should take care to wear warm clothing in winter. You are prone to illnesses and infections of the adrenals, kidneys, bladder, and sexual organs. Your tendency to be fretful and fearful can cause you extreme emotional distress and nervousness.

Decorating Guidelines

Your home should be arranged and decorated generally with rectangular shapes, smooth, flowing lines and patterns, rounded shapes, and the colors of Metal, Water, and Wood (white, silver, black, navy, midnight blue, light blue, and green).

Directions in Space

1 Water Star corresponds to north. The other directions in space that are in harmony with 1 Water are west, northwest, east, and southeast.

Stones, Plants, and Symbolic Associations

Stones for Water include black pebbles, stones from the ocean, corals, and stones from riverbeds.

Your plants include reeds, lilies, bulrushes, all water plants and plants that love water, such as willows, alders, and ashes, as well as all hanging plants and vines, and flowers that are nearly black in color.

Your symbolic associations are the heart, the moon, the abyss, rain, ice, a ravine, isolation, secrecy, pregnancy, danger, thieves, the pig.

The Basic Wood Personality

There are two Wood stars. The following attributes are applicable for both. Specific differences in other attributes are listed under the individual stars.

You are naturally kindhearted and practical. Of all the types, yours is the most ethical. You are also very decisive and an excellent problem solver. You are social, energetic, expansive, capable of handling many complex details at once and turning all you do to profit. Being something of a visionary, you love to make long-range plans. But when you get caught up in the future, and unexpected delays and complications come up, you lose patience and get angry.

When you are under too much stress and are in need of recuperation, the best place for you to go is to the woods or to the ocean.

DECORATING GUIDELINES

Your home should be decorated generally with rectangular shapes, smooth, flowing lines and patterns, beautiful displays of flowers and works of art, and with the colors of Water, Wood, and Fire (black, navy, midnight blue, light blue, greens, reds, pinks, and purples).

STONES AND PLANTS

The stones for Wood are blue and green, as well as those upon which lichens and moss grow.

Your plants are all the flowering trees, bamboo, grasses, pod-bearing plants, blue flowers, plants that grow luxuriantly, plants that send out runners and spread, such as wild strawberries, and flowers such as daisies, buttercups, poppies, and anemones.

3 WOOD STAR

Like the early spring with all its buds and flowers, you are full of surprises. You are naturally high-spirited, youthful, and naive. You are single-minded and capable of unswerving love and devotion. Gentleness is your greatest power and weakness. In your courageous way, which some think foolhardy, you tend to overreach your limits and meet all sorts of trials in life. You tend, when hurt or under too much pressure, to snap. You can resort to shouting, but, like a thunderstorm your anger soon passes and the air is clear and fresh.

You are full of plans and have all the energy in the world to bring them to fruition. Nonetheless, it is important for you to balance your habits of busyness with periods of rest and calm reflection.

OCCUPATIONS

You would do well as a writer, musician, designer, painter, photographer, filmmaker, teacher, computer engineer, electrical engineer, and in all occupations that call for planning and directing. You could do very well as a freelancer.

COMPATIBILITY

You are most compatible with 1 Water Star, 7 Metal Star, and 9 Fire Star, moderately compatible with 3 Wood Star and 4 Wood Star, and least compatible with 2 Earth Star, 5 Earth Star, 6 Metal Star, and 8 Earth Star.

HEALTH

You are blessed with excellent coordination, agility, and strength. Be careful to maintain the health of your liver and gallbladder. Avoid stimulants, drugs, and animal fats. You need periods of calm. Too much pressure and stress can, at worst, cause you mental and nervous illnesses.

DIRECTIONS IN SPACE

3 Wood corresponds to east. The other directions in space that are in harmony with 3 Wood are north, southeast, and south.

SYMBOLIC ASSOCIATIONS

Thunder, arousal, activity, advancement, promotion, rapid growth, springtime, blossoms, excitement, noise, musical instruments, surprises, the telephone, radio, stereo, television, computer, the dragon.

4 WOOD STAR

Like the wind, you need to move about and circulate. You are flexible and resilient. You have many interests. Being something of a wanderer, you tend to want to change residence rather often, to make numerous changes in your occupation, or to do two or more things at once.

Communication is very important to you, especially in your love relationships. Your ability to understand different sides at once makes you very tolerant of differences. You are gentle by nature and are gifted with penetrating insight. You live very much in a world of ideas and give positive value to learning and to sharing new information with your friends.

You tend to become worried about the future and plague yourself with doubts, which only causes you to change your mind over and over again, to procrastinate, and to miss your opportunities. Good fortune for you depends to a large degree on the sort of company you keep.

OCCUPATIONS

Favorable occupations for you are in the fields of communications, designing, furniture construction, writing, music, teaching, publishing, travel, shipping, postal service, diplomacy, and the lumber and paper industries.

COMPATIBILITY

You are most compatible with 1 Water Star, 6 Metal Star, and 9 Fire Star, moderately compatible with 3 Wood Star and 4 Wood Star, and least compatible with 2 Earth Star, 5 Earth Star, 7 Metal Star, and 8 Earth Star.

HEALTH

You are usually very active and energetic, and need to get a lot of fresh air to stay healthy. Be careful to maintain the health of your lungs and intestines and your immune function. You are very sensitive to airborne infections.

DIRECTIONS IN SPACE

4 Wood Star corresponds to southeast. The other directions in space that are in harmony with 4 Wood are north, east, and south.

SYMBOLIC ASSOCIATIONS

Wind, travel, advance and retreat, trade, transportation, distances, mail, post offices, telephone calls, rumors, birds, airplanes, marriage, the crane.

9 FIRE STAR

Like the sun, you love to rise and shine, and as the heart of Fire is dark and deep, you are something of a sphinx. A fountain of light, you are imaginative. You thrive in beautiful surroundings with fine and costly things. But because you may tend to become extravagant and live beyond your means, you can get yourself into trouble.

You have many friendly acquaintances, yet there are few in whom you ever place your trust. You are possessive and passionate. The loyalty and admiration of your loved one is essential for your happiness and well-being.

OCCUPATIONS

There are many occupations favorable for you as long as they are creative and self-expressive. You could be an artist, author, actor, inventor, politician, journalist, publisher, fashion designer, beautician, architectural and landscape designer, horticulturist.

COMPATIBILITY

You are most compatible with 1 Water Star, 2 Earth Star, 3 Wood Star, 4 Wood Star, 5 Earth Star, and 8 Earth Star, moderately compatible with 9 Fire Star, and least compatible with 6 Metal Star and 7 Metal Star.

HEALTH

Your health is very much affected by your emotions. If you are happy and blessed with love, you blossom. If you are beset with troubles, your digestion suffers, and you can develop heart problems, insomnia, and severe mental upsets.

DECORATING GUIDELINES

Your home should be cheerful, warmly decorated with rectangular and square shapes, radiant displays of flowers and works of art, and the colors of Wood, Fire, and Earth (light blue, greens, reds, pinks, purples, browns, beige, and yellows).

DIRECTIONS IN SPACE

9 Fire Star corresponds to south. The other directions in space that are in harmony with 9 Fire are east, southeast, southwest, and northeast.

STONES, PLANTS, AND SYMBOLIC ASSOCIATIONS

Stones for Fire are red, purple, sharp, and pointed.

Your plants are all those that have purple, pink, and red flowers, as well as red-leafed plants, maple trees, apple trees, heather, and red pepper plants.

The sun, summer, lightning, discovery, illumination, the eye, intellect, beauty, talent, knowledge, clinging, and the phoenix are your symbolic associations.

THE BASIC EARTH PERSONALITY

There are three Earth stars. The attributes below are applicable for all three of them. Specific differences follow.

It is your nature to protect and sustain life. You are self-reliant, independent, practical, and conservative, and have the aptitude to work hard and patiently build up a fortune. You are an efficient manager of your own and other people's resources and are attracted to real estate, the construction industry, medicine, the food industry, finance, and all forms of down-to-earth activities and services. You are methodical, careful, and detail oriented, and dislike doing more than one thing at a time. You have great reserves of energy and a capacity for endurance.

In your relationships you are responsive, steadfast, and supportive, while at the same time emotionally reserved and shy. You can be very sympathetic, and you go out of your way to offer practical help to those in need.

You are stubborn and resistant to change, and seriously ponder moves before making them.

DECORATING GUIDELINES

Your home should be very comfortable, decorated with square, round, and oval shapes, broad surfaces, and beautiful displays of flowers and works of art. You do best with the colors of Fire, Earth, and Metal (reds, pinks, purples, browns, beige, yellows, white, and silver).

STONES AND PLANTS

The stones corresponding to Earth are brown and yellow, square, broad, and flat.

Your trees and flowers include nut trees, mountain ash, pines, and mountain laurels; all bulb flowers such as tulips, irises, narcissuses, jonquils, and daffodils, and all yellow and orange flowers.

2 Earth Star

You are receptive and supportive, gentle, honest, and kindhearted. It is natural for you to tend to the needs of others and bring to completion what they have begun. As this is both your strength and weakness, you need to be careful that you do not yield to the pressures of those who would use you unfairly. You are essentially caring.

Occupations

You are suited to occupations in such areas as public service, social work, hospital work, nursing, farming, construction work, real estate, cooking, antiques, and gardening. It is easier for you to work for a boss than to be a boss. You work very efficiently as a member of a team, because you are essentially cooperative and thoroughly at home with others.

Compatibility

In love, you are attentive and devoted. You are also possessive and jealous, and have a big sexual appetite. You tend to be attracted to those older than yourself, or to those whose personalities are more forceful than yours.

You are most compatible with 6 Metal Star, 7 Metal Star, 8 Earth Star, and 9 Fire Star, moderately compatible with 2 Earth Star and 5 Earth Star, and least compatible with 1 Water Star, 3 Wood Star, and 4 Wood Star.

Health

To maintain good health, you have to be scientific about food and regulate your eating habits. You have a sweet tooth, which could be your downfall. You need to guard against diabetes, intestinal disorders, and blood disorders. It is very important for you to exercise—you tend to be too sedentary.

Directions in Space

2 Earth Star corresponds to southwest. The other directions in harmony with 2 Earth are west, northwest, northeast, and south.

SYMBOLIC ASSOCIATIONS

Valley, the mother, receptivity, supportiveness, patience, toil, frugality, endurance, obedience, farmers, laborers, the masses, fields, the prairie, wagons, kettles, cloth, the cow.

5 EARTH STAR

Although you are to all appearances shy and mild-mannered, you are, of all the Star types, the most stubborn and determined to have your way. It is either up or down for you. It is essential for you to be self-possessed and in control. The key to your well-being is to stay centered. If you allow yourself to become unbalanced, or taken too far out of your way, you fall. You can endure great hardships, if need be. You are a survivor.

As 5 Earth Star is pivotal, your life is full of turning points. You can also turn around the lives of the others who come into your world. You can get along with anyone and no one, depending on your mood, your central purpose being to assert your will. When your will is challenged, you tend to become suspicious and quarrelsome. It goes against your grain to follow anyone unless you find it to your ultimate advantage. You have the aptitude to become a leader and benefactor of society, and readily take on great responsibilities. You are very loyal to your parents and may become their primary caregiver in their later years.

OCCUPATIONS

You are suited to occupations in such areas as health care, corporate management, politics, law, the clergy, and any activity in which you can rise to a position of authority.

COMPATIBILITY

Although you might appear to be shy and even undemonstrative, you can become very demanding in love, as your need for acceptance is intense.

You are most compatible with 6 Metal Star, 7 Metal Star, and 9 Fire Star, moderately compatible with 2 Earth Star, 5 Earth Star, and 8 Earth Star, and least compatible with 1 Water Star, 3 Wood Star, and 4 Wood Star.

HEALTH

Although you are constitutionally strong, you can go to extremes at work and wear yourself down. It is good for you to balance work with some sort of recreation. You need to be careful to maintain the health of your heart and circulatory system, as well as your stomach.

DIRECTIONS IN SPACE

5 Earth Star corresponds to the middle. The directions in space that are in harmony with 5 Earth include west, northwest, northeast, southwest, and south.

SYMBOLIC ASSOCIATIONS

The North Star, the emperor, a pivot, a hinge, the center, the tortoise.

8 EARTH STAR

Opposite to the 2 Earth Star type who is at home in a group, you, like the mountain, stand alone. You are naturally reserved. Before deciding upon a course of action, you think very carefully. You take into account the minutest and most comprehensive details, and carefully weigh all pros and cons, so that once you make up your mind you are unlikely to change it. You are honest, reliable, and insightful, and inspire trust in others since you are capable of taking on great responsibilities.

OCCUPATIONS

You are hardworking and competitive in business, and can rise, like the mountain, to a place above all others. Your aptitudes lie in the fields of real estate, accounting, banking, business, education, medicine, social services, the clergy, architecture, and sculpting. With your ability to attract money, and to save and invest it wisely, you can amass a large fortune.

COMPATIBILITY

In love, you are protective and loyal, and work hard to provide your family with security and comfort.

You are most compatible with 2 Earth Star, 6 Metal Star, 7 Metal Star, and 9 Fire Star, moderately compatible with 5 Earth Star and 8 Earth Star, and least compatible with 1 Water Star, 3 Wood Star, and 4 Wood Star.

HEALTH

As your type tends toward becoming sedentary, you could develop chronic illness. It is very important for you to completely uproot illness at the outset. You need to be scientific about food intake and get regular exercise. You are prone to digestive and intestinal complaints and circulatory problems.

DIRECTIONS IN SPACE

8 Earth Star corresponds to northeast. The other directions in space that are in harmony with 8 Earth are south, southwest, west, and northwest.

SYMBOLIC ASSOCIATIONS

Mountain, mountain path, transition, stillness, vigil, watchman, monk, priest, sage, gateway, opening, crossroads, inheritance, new beginning, the dog.

THE BASIC METAL PERSONALITY

There are two metal stars. The attributes below are applicable for both. Specific differences follow.

You are essentially orderly and just, and you intuitively know what works and what doesn't. You are apt to set high standards for yourself and others, and become quite inflexible in your demands. You are faithful to your ideals and are self-motivated. You have strong directorial abilities, a positive sense of determination, excellent communication abilities, and powerful financial aptitudes.

When faced with difficulties you retreat into yourself, preferring your own counsel to that of others. Your single-mindedness can make quite a loner of you, and, if you cut yourself off, you can become sad and melancholy. You are proud to a fault. On the other hand, because you appreciate harmony and balanced order, you have excellent social skills and are most loyal and caring in love.

Decorating Guidelines

Your home should be elegant and neat. It should be decorated generally with square, round, and oval shapes, broad surfaces, flowing lines and patterns, and with the colors of Earth, Metal, and Water (yellows, beige, browns, white, silver, black, navy, and midnight blue).

Stones and Plants

The stones for Metal are white and gray, smooth and round.

Your plants and flowers include all fruit trees, trees that turn bright red in the fall, white flowers, chrysanthemums, and all fall flowers.

6 Metal Star

Like the sky that arches above the earth, it is natural for you to want to rise up above everything and everyone. Being idealistic and ambitious, you aim for the highest levels of spiritual development. You are straightforward and intuitive, and since you aim for the bird's-eye view, develop the ability to read the future. You are freedom-loving and willful, essentially intolerant of criticism. Your sense of self-esteem depends very much upon your ability to inspire and lead others. You are a perfectionist. You strive hard to reach your goals and expect the same of those around you.

Occupations

Suitable occupations for you are in such fields as government, law, education, the clergy, psychological and social counseling, communications, business management, sports, or any field that is both challenging and competitive, that gives you the opportunity to rise to an influential position in the world.

With your farsightedness and natural aptitudes for investing and organizing, you can build up a fortune and use it to promote the welfare and advancement of your family, friends, and community.

COMPATIBILITY

Out of sensitivity and concern, coupled with a strong sense of right and wrong, you can be very strict and demanding, if not overbearing, toward those you love.

You are most compatible with 2 Earth Star, 4 Wood Star, 5 Earth Star, and 8 Earth Star, moderately compatible with 1 Water Star, 6 Metal Star, and 7 Metal Star, and least compatible with 3 Wood Star and 9 Fire Star.

HEALTH

Because you are an extremely hard worker, you need to take care not to run yourself into the ground. To maintain your health, try to balance your work with exercise and rest, and be mindful of what you eat. You are vulnerable to diseases of the lungs and intestines, as well as the heart and the nervous system.

DIRECTIONS IN SPACE

6 Metal Star corresponds to northwest. The other directions in space that are in harmony with 6 Metal are southwest, west, north, and northeast.

SYMBOLIC ASSOCIATIONS

Heaven, the father, the creative, the prince, authority, harvest, jade, the horse.

7 METAL STAR

Imaginative and fun-loving, you like to entertain and be entertained. You are mild and elegant in manner, charming and sensitive, and have a natural aptitude to influence others. You are quick-witted, communicative, and optimistic, and very happy in partnership, both for business and in love.

You are strongly attracted to love and are most fortunate if you have a partner with whom you can communicate and share pleasures freely and openly. You are an artist of love. You enjoy what is most exquisite. Your partner should be as sociable as you, and his/her aims should be in perfect harmony with yours. You are blessed with the natural gift for negotiating that will always allow both you and your partner to act happily as equals. The world has much to learn from you in this respect.

If, on the other hand, you are not so fortunate and try to form a relationship with someone who is not responsive or willing to be open, you will sooner or later begin to react by becoming fickle and deceptive. You need to be careful not to confuse yourself; it could take you a long time to get back on track. The key to finding your way is to cultivate your beauty and self-esteem, and to be sincere. Be honest with yourself. You need a playmate.

OCCUPATIONS

Good occupations for you are in such areas as entertainment, the arts, communications, public relations, advertising, sales, teaching, banking, brokerage, and in resorts, hotels, restaurants, and bars.

COMPATIBILITY

You are most compatible with 2 Earth Star, 3 Wood Star, 5 Earth Star, and 8 Earth Star, moderately compatible with 1 Water Star, 6 Metal Star, and 7 Metal Star, and least compatible with 4 Wood Star and 9 Fire Star.

HEALTH

Because your senses are very alive, you need to cultivate a refined sense of aesthetics to maintain your health. You positively respond to fine perfumes, delicate tastes, beautiful art, fine clothing, and fine music. Excessive indulgence in sensual pleasures can lead to illnesses of the mouth, teeth, stomach, intestines, kidneys, and sexual organs.

DIRECTIONS IN SPACE

7 Metal Star corresponds to west. The other directions in space that are in harmony with 7 Metal are southwest, northwest, north, and northeast.

SYMBOLIC ASSOCIATIONS

The lake, running water, joyousness, pleasure, leisure, playfulness, parties, wine, dancing, singing, the mouth and tongue, the enchantress, the lovers, the sheep.

YOUR DOORWAY

Now that you know what your birth star is, let's find out whether it and the element of your doorway are in mutual harmony, and if they aren't, what you should do to create harmony between them.

Because your doorway faces one of the eight directions, it is aligned to one of the corresponding elements. The element of the direction to which your door is aligned is the element that rules your home. In other words, if your door faces **north**, your home is ruled by the element Water; if your door faces **northeast**, your home is ruled by the element Earth; if your door faces **east**, your home is ruled by the element Wood; if your door faces **southeast**, your home also is ruled by the element Wood; if your door faces **south**, your home is ruled by the element Fire; if your door faces **southwest**, your home is ruled by the element Earth; if your door faces **west**, your home is ruled by the element Metal; and if your door faces **northwest**, your home is again ruled by the element Metal.

Always read the door that separates your own living space from the outside world. For example, if you live in an apartment building the door to read is the entrance to your apartment, not the door of the building. If you own a house, the door to read is the main door, the door you habitually use. If you live in a room in a house or apartment, read the door of your room.

To determine the element of your doorway, take a compass reading of it. To do this, stand in the doorway, facing *out*. The direction you face on the compass indicates the door's element (see fig. 15 on page 34).

If you are uncertain of the direction you are facing, if it appears vague, or between two directions, figure 16 will help you determine it.

Looking at figure 16, you can see that north extends from 337.30 to 22.30; northeast from 22.30 to 67.30; east from 67.30 to 112.30; southeast from 112.30 to 157.30; south from 157.30 to 202.30; southwest from 202.30 to 247.30; west from 247.30 to 292.30; and northwest from 292.30 to 337.30.

(*fig. 16*)

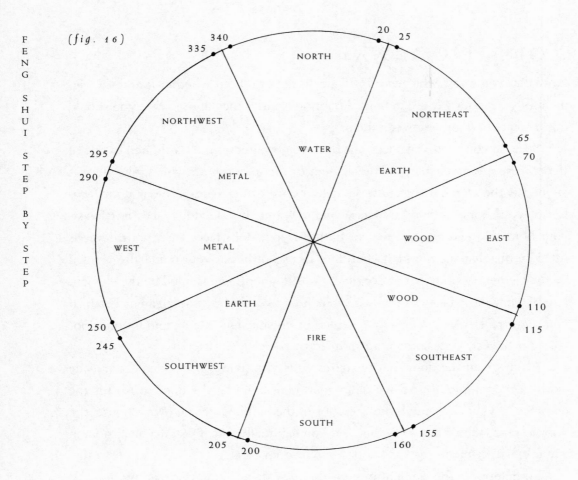

The following tables show the relations between the eight directions for a door and the nine birth stars. They also indicate the harmony and discord of the different combinations and what colors to use to create harmony.

If your situation indicates a need for a harmonizing color, you can:

- Paint the inside and/or outside of the door.
- Hang a picture on a wall adjacent to the door.
- Place a carpet in the foyer or entrance area near the door.
- Hang a wreath on the door.

Door Direction	Birth Star	Harmony/ Discord	Colors to Add for Harmony
North	1	Harmony	
	2	Discord	White
	3	Harmony	
	4	Harmony	
	5	Discord	White
	6	Harmony	
	7	Harmony	
	8	Discord	White
	9	Discord	Green or Blue
Northeast	1	Discord	White
	2	Harmony	
	3	Discord	Purple or Red
	4	Discord	Purple or Red
	5	Harmony	
	6	Harmony	
	7	Harmony	
	8	Harmony	
	9	Harmony	
East	1	Harmony	
	2	Discord	Purple or Red
	3	Harmony	
	4	Harmony	
	5	Discord	Purple or Red
	6	Discord	Black or Navy
	7	Discord	Black or Navy
	8	Discord	Purple or Red
	9	Harmony	
Southeast	1	Harmony	
	2	Discord	Purple or Red
	3	Harmony	
	4	Harmony	
	5	Discord	Purple or Red
	6	Discord	Black or Navy

DOOR DIRECTION	BIRTH STAR	HARMONY/ DISCORD	COLORS TO ADD FOR HARMONY
Southeast (*cont.*)	7	Discord	Black or Navy
	8	Discord	Purple or Red
	9	Harmony	
South	1	Discord	Green or Blue
	2	Harmony	
	3	Harmony	
	4	Harmony	
	5	Harmony	
	6	Discord	Yellow
	7	Discord	Yellow
	8	Harmony	
	9	Harmony	
Southwest	1	Discord	White
	2	Harmony	
	3	Discord	Purple or Red
	4	Discord	Purple or Red
	5	Harmony	
	6	Harmony	
	7	Harmony	
	8	Harmony	
	9	Harmony	
West	1	Harmony	
	2	Harmony	
	3	Discord	Black or Navy
	4	Discord	Black or Navy
	5	Harmony	
	6	Harmony	
	7	Harmony	
	8	Harmony	
	9	Discord	Yellow
Northwest	1	Harmony	
	2	Harmony	
	3	Discord	Black or Navy

DOOR DIRECTION	BIRTH STAR	HARMONY/ DISCORD	COLORS TO ADD FOR HARMONY
Northwest (*cont.*)	4	Discord	Black or Navy
	5	Harmony	
	6	Harmony	
	7	Harmony	
	8	Harmony	
	9	Discord	Yellow

You can harmonize your birth star not only with the front door, but with the door of each and every room in your house. Remember: to find the correct door direction, look *out*, not in.

EXERCISES

1. *If you have not already done so, enter in your personal data list:*
   - Your birth star
   - The direction in space that corresponds to your birth star
   - The other directions in space that are in harmony with your birth star
   - The decoration themes (lines and shapes) and colors that relate to your birth star
2. *Write down:*
   - The compass direction of your doorway
   - The harmony or discord of your birth star with your door's direction
   - The color to use at your doorway if your birth star and your door's direction are discordant
3. *If you live with someone else, write:*
   - His/her birth star with its corresponding directions in space, decoration themes, and colors
   - The harmony and discord of his/her birth star with the door's direction
   - The color to use at the doorway if his/her birth star is out of harmony with the door's direction

YOUR MUTUALLY HARMONIOUS STARS

You can arrange and decorate your home to accommodate and support all who live there according to the coordinates of your mutually harmonious stars, as shown below.

For example, if two people live together, and one of them is 1 Water Star and the other is 2 Earth Star, they have 6 and 7 Metal Stars in common. Therefore they can align their bed either to the west or northwest. The colors white and silver will harmonize with them, and they can accent the decor of their home with the smooth, round, and oval shapes and patterns indicated by Metal.

BIRTH STARS		MUTUALLY HARMONIOUS STARS
PERSON 1	PERSON 2	
1	1	1, 3, 4, 6, 7
1	2	6, 7
1	3	1, 3, 4, 9
1	4	1, 3, 4, 9
1	5	6, 7
1	6	1, 6, 7
1	7	1, 6, 7
1	8	6, 7
1	9	3, 4

BIRTH STARS		MUTUALLY HARMONIOUS STARS
PERSON 1	PERSON 2	
2	2	2, 6, 7, 8, 9
2	3	9
2	4	9
2	5	2, 6, 7, 8, 9
2	6	2, 6, 7, 8
2	7	2, 6, 7, 8
2	8	2, 6, 7, 8, 9
2	9	2, 8, 9
3	3	1, 3, 4, 9
3	4	1, 3, 4, 9
3	5	9
3	6	1
3	7	1
3	8	9
3	9	3, 4, 9
4	4	1, 3, 4, 9
4	5	9
4	6	1
4	7	1
4	8	9
4	9	3, 4, 9
5	5	2, 6, 7, 8, 9
5	6	2, 6, 7, 8
5	7	2, 6, 7, 8
5	8	2, 6, 7, 8, 9
5	9	2, 8, 9
6	6	1, 2, 6, 7, 8
6	7	1, 2, 6, 7, 8
6	8	2, 6, 7, 8
6	9	2, 8
7	7	1, 2, 6, 7, 8
7	8	2, 6, 7, 8

BIRTH STARS		MUTUALLY HARMONIOUS STARS
PERSON 1	PERSON 2	
7	9	2, 8
8	8	2, 6, 7, 8
8	9	2, 8, 9
9	9	2, 3, 4, 8, 9

If three people live together and the first is 2 Earth Star, the second is 4 Wood Star, and the third is 9 Fire Star, they all have 9 Fire Star in common. Therefore the colors red and purple will harmonize with them, and their home can be accented with the radiant patterns and brilliant displays of flowers and works of art indicated by Fire.

The more people you have living together the fewer chances you will have to find mutually harmonious stars. However, you can arrange and decorate your home to accommodate everyone according to the coordinates of an element that might be needed to complete the cycle of the five elements.

For example, four people are living together. The first is 1 Water Star, the second is 2 Earth Star, the third is 3 Wood Star, and the fourth is 9 Fire Star. If we arrange their birth stars in a chart we can easily find the element that is needed to complete the cycle with them:

	1 WATER	2 EARTH	3 WOOD	9 FIRE
1 Water	.	6 and 7 Metal	4 Wood	3 and 4 Wood
2 Earth		.	9 Fire	8 Earth
3 Wood			.	4 Wood
9 Fire				.

If you look closely, you will see that the elements represented by the four people, Water, Earth, Wood, and Fire, need Metal to complete the cycle. Therefore, the colors, shapes, and patterns of Metal should be emphasized in their home.

When several people live together, you should also judge the birth star of each against the element of the doorway, and for whomever you find disharmony, add the appropriate color for harmony on or near the door.

EXERCISES

If you live with someone else, list on your personal data page:

- Your mutually harmonious stars
- The directions in space that correspond to your mutually harmonious stars
- The decoration themes (lines and shapes) and colors that relate to your mutually harmonious stars

YOUR LUCKY STARS: THE KEY TO YOUR PERSONAL STYLE

Now that you have figured out your birth star and understand how it works in the nine star system, you're ready to refine your calculations further by pinpointing your lucky stars. Your lucky stars will help you learn more about your own unique personal style by indicating your most favorable directions in space, your most auspicious—or lucky—colors, and your best shapes and patterns.

The lucky stars are listed in a table below. Please note that there is one calculation for males and another for females. In both cases, the calculation is based on the year and month of birth.

You will recall that the Chinese solar year begins on February 4th. The corresponding months have no names, but are assigned numbers 1 through 12. With their equivalent Western dates, they are as follows:

CHINESE MONTH	EQUIVALENT WESTERN DATES
1	February 4th through March 4th
2	March 5th through April 4th
3	April 5th through May 4th
4	May 5th through June 5th
5	June 6th through July 6th

Chinese Month	Equivalent Western Dates
6	July 7th through August 6th
7	August 7th through September 6th
8	September 7th through October 7th
9	October 8th through November 6th
10	November 7th through December 6th
11	December 7th through January 4th
12	January 5th through February 3rd

In order to find your lucky star numbers, follow this procedure:

1. Find your birth star number on your personal data list.
2. Note the Chinese month in which you were born, as shown above.
3. Find and note your month star number using the tables below (one for males and one for females). Find your birth star number at the left of the table, and find your Chinese month at the top of the table. Your month star number is located where the birth star row and the month star column meet.
4. Using your birth star number and month star number, look up your lucky star numbers in the table for lucky stars.

Month Stars for Males

Chinese Month	1	2	3	4	5	6	7	8	9	10	11	12
Birth Star 1,4,7	8	7	6	5	4	3	2	1	9	8	7	6
3,6,9	5	4	3	2	1	9	8	7	6	5	4	3
2,5,8	2	1	9	8	7	6	5	4	3	2	1	9

For example, if you are a male born under 1 Water Star, during the first Chinese month, you have 8 Earth Star as your month star.

If you are a male born under 6 Metal Star, during the eighth Chinese month, your month star is 7 Metal Star.

63

MONTH STARS FOR FEMALES

CHINESE MONTH	1	2	3	4	5	6	7	8	9	10	11	12
BIRTH STAR 5,2,8	7	8	9	1	2	3	4	5	6	7	8	9
3,9,6	1	2	3	4	5	6	7	8	9	1	2	3
4,1,7	4	5	6	7	8	9	1	2	3	4	5	6

Thus, if you are a female born under 7 Metal Star in the seventh Chinese month, your month star is 1 Water Star.

Remember, the elements of the stars are 1 Water, 2 Earth, 3 Wood, 4 Wood, 5 Earth, 6 Metal, 7 Metal, 8 Earth, 9 Fire.

Now that you know your month star, combine it with your birth star, using the table below, and you will discover your lucky stars.

YOUR LUCKY STARS

BIRTH STAR	MONTH STAR	LUCKY STARS
1	1	3, 4, 6, 7
1	2	6, 7
1	3	4
1	4	3
1	5	6, 7
1	6	7
1	7	6
1	8	6, 7
1	9	3, 4
2	1	6, 7
2	2	5, 6, 7, 8, 9
2	3	9
2	4	9
2	5	6, 7, 8
2	6	5, 7, 8
2	7	5, 6, 8

Birth Star	Month Star	Lucky Stars
2	8	5, 6, 7, 9
2	9	5, 8
3	1	4
3	2	9
3	3	1, 4, 9
3	4	1, 9
3	5	9
3	6	1
3	7	1
3	8	9
3	9	4
4	1	3
4	2	9
4	3	1, 9
4	4	1, 3, 9
4	5	9
4	6	1
4	7	1
4	8	9
4	9	3
5	1	6, 7
5	2	6, 7, 8, 9
5	3	9
5	4	9
5	5	2, 6, 7, 8, 9
5	6	2, 7, 8
5	7	2, 6, 8
5	8	2, 6, 7
5	9	2, 8
6	1	7
6	2	5, 7, 8
6	3	1
6	4	1
6	5	2, 7, 8

Birth Star	Month Star	Lucky Stars
6	6	1, 2, 5, 7, 8
6	7	1, 2, 5, 8
6	8	2, 5, 7
6	9	2, 5, 8
7	1	6
7	2	5, 6, 8
7	3	1
7	4	1
7	5	2, 6, 8
7	6	1, 2, 5, 8
7	7	1, 2, 5, 6, 8
7	8	2, 5, 6
7	9	2, 5, 8
8	1	6, 7
8	2	5, 6, 7, 9
8	3	9
8	4	9
8	5	2, 6, 7, 9
8	6	2, 5, 7
8	7	2, 5, 6
8	8	2, 5, 6, 7, 9
8	9	2, 5
9	1	3, 4
9	2	5, 8
9	3	4
9	4	3
9	5	2, 8
9	6	2, 5, 8
9	7	2, 5, 8
9	8	2, 5
9	9	2, 3, 4, 5, 8

LUCKY STAR COLOR SCALE

Here is a special color scale to use only in connection with your lucky stars. Use your lucky colors to focus your personal style. The lucky colors are as follows:

STAR	COLOR
1 Water Star	white
2 Earth Star	black
3 Wood Star	jade green
4 Wood Star	green
5 Earth Star	yellow
6 Metal Star	white
7 Metal Star	red
8 Earth Star	white
9 Fire Star	purple

List your lucky star or stars, their corresponding special colors, their corresponding directions in space (north for 1 Water, southwest for 2 Earth, east for 3 Wood, southeast for 4 Wood, middle for 5 Earth, northwest for 6 Metal, west for 7 Metal, northeast for 8 Earth, south for 9 Fire), and their corresponding shapes and patterns (smooth, flowing, asymmetrical forms and patterns for 1 Water; broad, flat, square forms and patterns for 2 Earth, 5 Earth, and 8 Earth; rectangular forms and patterns for 3 Wood and 4 Wood; smooth, round, and oval forms and patterns for 6 Metal and 7 Metal; radiant patterns and cheerful displays of flowers and works of art for 9 Fire) on your personal data sheet.

Here are a few examples to demonstrate how lucky stars are interpreted:

1. A male born on May 30, 1964, has 9 Fire Star as his birth star and 2 Earth Star as his month star. Therefore 5 Earth Star and 8 Earth Star are his lucky stars. The corresponding spatial directions for his lucky stars are the middle for 5 Earth and northeast for 8 Earth; his lucky colors are yellow and white; and his most favorable shapes and patterns are broad, flat, and square, which correspond to Earth.

2. A female born on May 30, 1964, has 6 Metal Star as her birth star and 4 Wood Star as her month star. Therefore 1 Water Star is her lucky star. The corresponding spatial direction for her lucky star is north; her lucky color is white; and her most favorable shapes and patterns are smooth, flowing, and asymmetrical, which correspond to Water.

3. A male born on July 17, 1953, has 2 Earth Star as his birth star and 6 Metal Star as his month star. Therefore 5 Earth Star, 7 Metal Star, and 8 Earth Star are his lucky stars. The corresponding spatial directions for his lucky stars are the middle for 5 Earth, west for 7 Metal, and northeast for 8 Earth; his lucky colors are yellow, red, and white; and his most favorable shapes and patterns are broad, flat, and square, as well as round and oval, which correspond to Earth and Metal.

To arrange and decorate your home according to a combination of your lucky stars and those of one or more other people, check to see if you have lucky stars in common. If not, plan your space using your mutually harmonious stars as found in chapter 6. It might be that one of those is also a lucky star for one of you.

EXERCISES

1. *If you have not done so yet, write in your list of personal data:*
   - Your lucky star or stars
   - The directions in space that correspond to your lucky stars
   - The special colors for your lucky stars
   - The corresponding decoration themes (shapes and patterns) for your lucky stars

2. If you live with someone else, write down his/her lucky stars with their corresponding directions in space, special colors, and corresponding decoration themes.

Before you make final decisions about your color scheme and the alignment of your bed and other articles of furniture, please wait until you have read Part 2 of this book in its entirety. Don't skip.

THE FORTUNE OF
YOUR DOOR

The door is important because it reveals something about the conditions you experience while living in your home. If you wish to find out what your door presages, you need only to combine your birth star with the compass direction of your door. Remember, the compass direction is the direction you face when you stand in the doorway with your back to the inside of your home, facing out.

Use the table of door and birth star combinations below and find your fortune as indicated by the number where the horizontal Door column and the vertical Star column meet. For example, if your door looks to the east, and your birth star number is 6, you would read paragraph 21 in the fortunes that follow.

Although the prognostications are not engraved in stone, they do have relevant meanings. Read them only in their most positive and constructive sense. If you are cautioned or warned of difficulty, for example, remember that you are always given the opportunity to find ways of overcoming possible hardship. And remember what Confucious said: "The way out is through the door. Strange how so few people use this method."

You will notice that in this system 5 Star is not listed among the stars in the table. Males born under 5 Star should use 2 Star; females born under 5 Star should use 8 Star. For example, a male born under 5 Star whose door faces south should read paragraph 34; a female born under 5 Star whose door looks south should read paragraph 39.

Door and Birth Star Combinations

Birth Stars:		1	2	3	4	6	7	8	9
Door Faces:	North	1	2	3	4	5	6	7	8
	Northeast	9	10	11	12	13	14	15	16
	East	17	18	19	20	21	22	23	24
	Southeast	25	26	27	28	29	30	31	32
	South	33	34	35	36	37	38	39	40
	Southwest	41	42	43	44	45	46	47	48
	West	49	50	51	52	53	54	55	56
	Northwest	57	58	59	60	61	62	63	64

Fortunes

1.   IMAGE: *walking at the edge of an icy precipice at midnight without a light*

You will be confronted by all that you fear. Be on guard against serious entanglements, which will surely lead to emotional upset and loss of money. Confusion can occur and cloud your mind. Heedlessness to good counsel will needlessly expose you to danger. Take care and avoid bad moves. Develop vigilance. Wait until the dawn; wait until you clearly see the way. Then act. By following your desire you will develop wisdom. If you are a writer, you will be fortunate here.

2.   IMAGE: *an incongruous gathering of people where conflicts arise*

Interference hinders progress. Scheming and quarreling lead to separations and losses. Issues about giving and receiving emotional and material support need to be sorted out. Remain true to your highest ideals. Be on guard against trickery. New ventures will run into complications. If you are circumspect and avoid confiding in the wrong people, you will become successful. Be aware of what you want and what you are attracting.

3.   IMAGE: *a remote cabin in the woods*

If you experience difficulties and setbacks, be patient; favorable changes will come about in due time. Your home favors leisure more than professional ambition. Financial prospects may not be the best, but you will have what you need to make ends meet. Be on guard against envy. Gossip will lead to trouble and disrepute. Contentment is your greatest wealth.

4.   IMAGE: *a traveler retreating from a hazardous pass in the mountains*

You are blessed with divine protection. If you cultivate a humanitarian attitude and are willing to be of service to others, you will enjoy unobstructed growth, prosperity, and a good reputation. If, on the other hand, you are selfishly ambitious, you will come to a dangerous impasse. If you are running into more and more complications in your life, retreat and examine your motives.

5.   IMAGE: *water being poured from a golden vessel*

Good fortune will flow to you as if from heaven. Success will come no matter what you do. It will be especially auspicious if you provide a needed service. You will benefit by creating opportunities for others. Seek the cooperation of friends.

6.   IMAGE: *a fresh stream of water flowing down from a lake into a valley*

Your fortunes will flourish. It is wise to follow your desires conservatively. Be careful when making changes. It will be to your advantage to define and maintain your boundaries. Don't bite off more than you can chew.

7.   IMAGE: *a waterfall cascading from the face of a towering rocky mountain into a rich green forest*

Difficulties eventually give way to good fortune. There is much hope for you here. Be patient. If you hold out against untoward circumstances, you will come to enjoy great and lasting prosperity. Seek out ways to bring the diverging elements in your life into harmony. If you let others help you, your aims for prosperity and success will be realized.

8.   IMAGE: *a field, rich with corn, under the afternoon sun*

Timely efforts bring rich rewards. Early stages of new ventures will be difficult, but after the midpoint, fortunes will flourish. Proceed calmly and carefully. Rely on experts for help and advice. You will overcome the challenges you face by focused attention and hard work. When your efforts are at maximum intensity, you will break through and your creative ideas will bear fruit. Great happiness will come to you and those you love.

9.   IMAGE: *a spring concealed in a mountain*

A lonely place. If you are peaceful and content with simplicity and quietly develop your talents, your life will come to flourish. Be adaptable and patient. Obstinacy and impatience will only lead to failure. Your creative ideas and efforts will bear rich fruit in time. The goodness of your intentions will insure lasting success.

10.   IMAGE: *inherited wealth*

Good fortune and abundance will come to you if you cultivate a cooperative attitude. Be mindful of the relatedness of all life. The spirit of ancestors comes through to you very strongly here. They offer you the blessings of long life, prosperity, and many descendants.

11.   IMAGE: *a field lying fallow*

You will experience difficult beginnings. Forcing your way will only lead to misfortune. If you call up your best powers of insight, however, you will find what you need to succeed. Don't overlook the possibility that the difficulties you experience are actually caused by the way you view the world. If you discover your hidden talents and untapped resources, good fortune will follow. With the help of good people, you will become prosperous and even famous, and in the long run you will be able to share your good fortune with many others.

12. IMAGE: *a wanderer lost in steep mountains and dense fog*
If, in the face of difficulties, you give in to desperate struggling, you will only get lost. Rash actions will be the cause of much regret. Be aware of your mistakes and avoid becoming intolerant. Be courageous and let go of harmful thoughts. You will attract powerful friends and powerful enemies. Good fortune will be attained if you cultivate the patience to wait out difficult periods and if you are very discriminating and conscientious in your actions.

13. IMAGE: *suspended animation*
If you fall into the aimlessness this place suggests, there will be little or no progress in your career and your relationships will tend to stagnate. If, on the other hand, you want to make progress, you will have to overcome inertia. Concentrate and persevere at your work. As activities increase, so will your responsibilities. Luck comes with discipline.

14. IMAGE: *a mirror-like pond in wooded mountains*
Cultivate balanced social relations and an easy manner and you will receive the help you need to become prosperous. Business and artistic activities will succeed if you enter them in partnership. If you are alone, you will find a companion. Marriage is favored. If, on the other hand, you decide to go it alone, your friendships will tend to come undone, progress will be slow, and money will be scarce. In the end, however, your fortunes will take a turn for the better.

15. IMAGE: *a gold mine in a mountain*
Being tranquil, like the mountain, you will be able to attain wealth, health, and happiness. Tranquillity is the result of exercising inner stillness. Staying calm and centered, skillfully handling all that comes to you, will insure steady growth and progress. Like the earth that produces gold, your strong and constant efforts will result in lasting abundance for you and your loved ones.

16. IMAGE: *the descending order of the generations—the grandmother, the mother and the daughter, the grandfather, the father and the son*

Step by step you will attain all of your objectives. Be at peace with your lot. Cultivate your talents and do whatever needs to be done. Live simply and avoid being ostentatious; you will rise surely and steadily. You will become prosperous, life will go more and more smoothly, and all that you truly desire will be realized.

17. IMAGE: *a sparkling river flowing in a luxuriant wood*

Great good fortune and happiness await you in this place. If you are looking for a mate, you will be very lucky. If you are contemplating marriage, the outlook is excellent. If you follow the golden rule, you will come to occupy a central place and be an inspiration to others. Your creative efforts will meet with success and money will flow to you. The more selfless you become, the happier you will be.

18. IMAGE: *the woods blossoming in the springtime*

You will enjoy abundant growth and prosperity if you rely more on the help of those in higher positions than on your own efforts. Be careful not to boast, however; it betrays weakness and causes you trouble. Good fortune will come through new or renewed ventures and through ventures that start out small but have the potential of becoming large. You may receive a windfall.

19. IMAGE: *thunder and wind*

Everything will flourish. Help will come to you from those in high places and from unexpected sources. Be clear about your goals and wait for the right time to act. Whatever you truly want, you will attain. Prosperity, good health, and happiness will be yours. By all means strive for improvements in life, but don't force it. Be on guard against trouble that comes up suddenly. If it does, stay calm and detached; it will pass.

20. IMAGE: *a sunset in the late autumn*

Strive to bring long-range plans and projects to completion. Put your roots down and grow. The grass is not greener on the other side. If you are doubtful and inconsistent, you will risk financial misfortune and marital troubles. If you perse-vere in bringing things to their natural fulfillment, you will enjoy great good for-tune. If you hope to marry, the outlook is highly favorable. Be willing, however, to make necessary sacrifices.

21. IMAGE: *a falling star*

In times of trouble, don't overuse power. Be on guard against unforeseen dan-gers. Don't take anything at face value. Appearances may be deceiving. Working out plans and making decisions under such elusive conditions spells trouble. Why shoot at a target that simply isn't there? Better wait and cultivate your powers of observation. Everything changes. If you are patient, you will eventually be able to make unobstructed progress and attain your goals.

22. IMAGE: *wood being chopped and thrown into a fire*

First you will experience difficulties, but then success will come. In difficult times, ambitious plans will be impossible to achieve and you may suffer dis-credit. You may experience difficulties in marriage as well. Be on guard against infidelity in love. Avoid mistrust and restlessness. You will get nowhere using the wrong methods. Wait for the right moment to take positive action; you will have a breakthrough. Opportunities for prosperity and happiness in love will then abound.

23. IMAGE: *a lotus-eater*

How can you expect to live by daydreaming, which brings only mediocre financial prospects? You will be fortunate if you cultivate humility. Be flexible, temperate in judgment, and willing to be of service to others. Useful opportunities will then come to you. If you take advantage of them, you will prosper.

24. IMAGE: *a thunderstorm*

Take advantage of expert help. Heedless and aggressive pursuit of your aims may result in collapse. You are in danger of wasting much time, energy, and money. Cultivate self-restraint and powers of discrimination. Be flexible. The cause of your difficulties lies within yourself. By blaming others, you miss the opportunity for positive change. If you get expert help, you will be able to rise to a high place and become prosperous.

25. IMAGE: *a ship in danger of running aground*

Don't take your luck for granted. Conditions are changeable. It will be to your advantage to be adaptable. Keep a sharp lookout and be prepared to deal intelligently with obstacles. Know when to retreat and when to advance. You will arrive at your destination sooner by making allowances for delays than by forcing your way. If you work for the benefit of others, you will attract good fortune. Play your cards right and you will enjoy increasing prosperity, good health, and a good reputation.

26. IMAGE: *a rich green valley*

You will enjoy abundant growth and prosperity if you work hard to attain knowledge. Cultivate loyalty. Good fortune will come to you through new ventures and through ventures that start out small but have the potential to grow large. To realize your full potential, broaden your outlook, be faithful to your family and community, and promote the universal good.

27. IMAGE: *a dragon appearing in a whirlwind*

Everything flourishes. Help will come to you from unusual sources. You may gain through adverse circumstances, especially if you seek out opportunities to serve others. Whatever you truly want, you will attain. Be energetic and keep high ideals. You will advance to a high position, become prosperous, and enjoy good health and love. Be on guard against insincerity, however, for it will bring misfortune.

28. IMAGE: *the wind rustling through the trees*

It is unwise to be distrustful. Avoid becoming suspicious and meddlesome. Your affairs will flourish if you guard against tendencies to be indecisive and impractical.

Help will come to you from people in high places. Protect yourself against useless hardships and concentrate on your personal development. Whatever you truly want, you will be able to attain. Anxious questioning is a waste of time.

29. IMAGE: *a bodhisattva, a practitioner of selfless compassion*

Many obstacles will come your way. You will be challenged again and again to search yourself and to tap your deepest resources and latent talents. Don't give in to tendencies to isolate yourself and become despondent. Follow your intuition. Help comes unexpectedly. Trust your innate sense of right and wrong. You will come to no harm. As you conquer your obstructions, you will become able to be of real help to others.

30. IMAGE: *a castle falling to ruin*

Humility and selfless devotion are auspicious. If you take responsibility for the trust others place in you, you will advance in life. On the other hand, insincerity and irresponsibility will cause you to undermine your career and personal relationships. Aggressive pursuit of selfish aims in troubled times will only compound trouble. It is better to retreat. Cultivate right conduct and honesty. Everything changes in time. If you exercise patience, your fortunes will improve.

31. IMAGE: *a mountain covered with trees that are all in flames*

Inconsideration and reckless action lead to rifts. You will meet with professional opposition as well as troubles at home. Be on guard against tendencies to be indifferent toward loved ones. Keep faith during trying times and learn from your mistakes. Be vigilant. Timely action will result in good fortune. Take advantage of unexpected opportunities. You may receive help from someone in a high place. The door to whatever path you wish to take will open.

32. IMAGE: *a woman tending a fire*

For you, life at home is more pleasant than the ups and downs of life out in the world in pursuit of fame and fortune. Be receptive and attentive. You will be very fortunate if you enjoy helping others. If you work creatively at home, you will prosper. Home is especially conducive to love, good health, and a happy family life.

33. IMAGE: *a pioneer*

Complications rooted in past mistakes may force you to start anew. Don't overestimate your knowledge and skills. There is much to learn. Follow the example of others who have more expertise than you, and the way to prosperity, happiness, and good health will open. Be patient when under pressure. Hold to that which nourishes your spirit.

34. IMAGE: *the sun setting over a scorched desert*

Venturing forth under adverse conditions will bring you nothing but loss. It is better to wait for conditions to change. Take advantage of periods of waiting by broadening your mental horizons. Carefully examine the inner causes of your difficulties and guard against blaming others. In due time you will be able to take creative action. The way will open and you will prosper.

35. IMAGE: *the myriad life forms that are embodied in the earth*

Abundant opportunities for progress and prosperity come to your door. You are blessed by heaven with unobstructed creativity. You have luck and are able to turn negative conditions into positive ones, not only for yourself, but for others as well. Helping others draws down the blessings of heaven. If you follow the golden rule, you will be highly respected.

36. IMAGE: *a brilliant star*

What you believe in your heart will come true. Cultivate positive faith, concentrate your efforts, and you will succeed in realizing every one of your aims. Abundant opportunities lie before you. Good health, professional success, and a good reputation come to your door. With patience and intelligent planning, you will be able to build a fortune that will provide comfort and security not only to you and your loved ones, but to future generations as well.

37. IMAGE: *an initiation ceremony, a transmission of light*

It will be a challenge to be receptive and humble. If you hold an egoistic attitude and insist upon being the leader, not only will you miss the point but you will be depleted. Let go. Be open in order to receive creative inspiration. Let yourself join forces with others. Be cooperative and flexible. You will be respected for your talents.

38. IMAGE: *a recluse*

When roads are closed, it is better to return to old conditions and wait. Be on guard against the lure of unrealistic schemes. Take advantage of periods of inactivity by gaining more knowledge. The greater your knowledge, the greater your chances for ultimate success. You will be helped by your superiors. If you are alone, you will meet someone in whom you will be able to place your trust. Good fortune will come through a companion.

39. IMAGE: *a sunset over the mountains*

The past looks better than the future in some important respects. The future seems to have limited prospects. You may be neglecting an important aspect of your life. Cultivate insight and examine your needs. It is useless to dwell on the past and blame others for your troubles. Observe decorum and generosity of spirit or you will suffer losses. Cultivate seriousness of purpose. You will be successful in occupations that involve research and investigation.

40. IMAGE: *water rising to the boiling point*

Advance, don't retreat. Strive to know your true aim and seize your opportunities as they show up. Be on guard against becoming distracted, and don't be afraid to take corrective measures when necessary. Conditions may change swiftly. You will need to be alert and ready to make quick and expedient decisions. Keep your goal clearly before you and you will have surprising success.

41. IMAGE: *a spearhead*

Persevere in going forward. To avoid danger is worse in the long run than exposure. If you lack courage and leadership skills, you will suffer losses. You will be confronted by much uncertainty, doubt, and frustration. If you turn tail and run away, however, you will meet with disaster. You have no choice but to press forward and cultivate new skills as you go along. Be resolute.

42. IMAGE: *a gold mine deep in a valley*

You will be more fortunate by following than leading. Be responsive to others and you will live a full and satisfying life. Stay calm and centered, skillfully manage your affairs, and steady progress and growth is assured. Like the earth that produces gold, your strong and constant efforts will result in lasting abundance for you and those whom you love.

43. IMAGE: *a farmer laboring under adverse conditions in springtime*

Do not succumb to doubts or let early failures discourage you. Strive patiently to overcome obstacles. Weakness will be followed by strength. If you are adaptable and hardworking, you will attract the help of people in high places. Creative projects will ultimately bear rich fruit.

44. IMAGE: *breaking ground and striking gold*

Hardships are followed by gains. Be adaptable. Persevere and you will overcome obstacles. If you display courage and positive determination, you will attract the support of superiors and will eventually attain a high position. You will strike gold through creative activities.

45. IMAGE: *a mirror*

To go forward is to go back. If you find conditions in the world unsatisfactory, recognize the deficiency in yourself. Return to the peace and security of your home and cultivate your talents. If you persevere, you will ultimately become successful. You will receive needed help from friendly people. Creative freelance work is most favorable. Later years will be easy.

46. IMAGE: *people playing tug of war*

Creating is confused with destroying. Guard against acting at cross-purposes with yourself. Don't waste your time minding other people's business. Be aware of what you are creating. If you are discerning, you will discover many interesting opportunities for your own advancement and prosperity, and for creating peaceful conditions at home.

47. IMAGE: *blessings coming down from honored ancestors*

You will attract good fortune by adopting a modest attitude. Cultivate friendly relations with neighbors. Be mindful of the relatedness of all life. The spirits of ancestors come through very powerfully for you here. They offer you their blessings of long life, prosperity, and many descendants. Everything points toward success.

48. IMAGE: *rearing a child*

You need patience. Success depends on biding your time and acting at the right moment. Be kind to yourself. Rest and cultivate good health. You will be prosperous and fortunate in your marriage and raising your children.

49. IMAGE: *a mirage*

Examine possible discrepancies between what you imagine and what actually exists. Gains may be ephemeral. Be circumspect. What appear to be opportunities may actually lead to reversals. Take advantage of inactive periods by attaining new knowledge. Be very discriminating, persevere in what you know to be right, and you will be successful.

50. IMAGE: *a ruby flashing in the sunlight*

Fame comes with successful works. Let your intuition guide your decisions about possible courses of action. Specialize in your field of endeavor and prosperity and renown will be yours. Take advantage of the help of juniors or people under you, but show care and consideration for them. Your good fortune will be long-lasting.

51. IMAGE: *navigating a ship by the stars*

You will be successful by following your true aim or potential. If you're not aware of your true course in life, spend time exploring various routes until you discover it. Once found, devote your full attention to its fulfillment. Seeking new knowledge will always be of great benefit to you. Your success depends on self-cultivation. Know what you need. Be cautious and discriminating. Don't waste time with the wrong people.

52. IMAGE: *an underground lake*

What you seek will be out of reach unless obstacles are removed. There will be very few to help you and you will have trouble finding companionship. Your growth will be limited unless you tap your own resources. Seek to discover your inner strengths and talents. Once you achieve self-knowledge, think and act independently, and use your talents for the benefit of others, you will be prosperous, well-known, and fortunate in love.

53. IMAGE: *the chopping down of a forest*

Curbing evil brings rich rewards. The beginning may be lucky, but incompetence and extreme actions will threaten ruin. Follow the middle way. Strengthen your spirit and sense of purpose, and analyze your situation before deciding on the best course of action. Be careful about whom you employ. Preserve early gains, be moderate, and rely on expert advice.

54. IMAGE: *an island in a garden pond*

Worldly pleasures will be yours. What you desire, you will get. Take advantage of your opportunities. You will be helped by someone in a high place as well as by your peers. Your fortunes will flourish. Beware of vanity, however.

55. IMAGE: *a mountain lake reflecting the heavens*

Whose ideas are you following? Slavishly following the rules of others is unfortunate. If you cultivate independence, you will attain your goals. Your creative possibilities are endless. Tireless effort will bring about great productivity, wealth, good fortune in love, and a healthy and happy family.

56. IMAGE: *gold being refined by fire*

Though hardships have to be endured, they are followed by flourishing fortunes. Work hard to clearly define your aims. Develop managerial skills in both professional and personal affairs. Change brings promotion, resulting in a secure position. Before you set out to reform others, however, work to refine yourself.

57. IMAGE: *the sun shining at midnight*

If you are timorous and self-centered, you will be used by others and will have to work hard for small gains. Abandon selfishness and expand your life. You will discover where you are genuinely useful if you cultivate inner light and follow your intuition. Be gentle and promote peace and harmony. Success will come through cooperation. Accept divine guidance.

58. IMAGE: *the gulf between heaven and earth*

Do not attempt to achieve something beyond your abilities or qualifications. Work at improving your skills if you don't want to be held back. Serious lessons in life may have to be learned in order to overcome misfortunes. Follow your heart. Once you develop the skills you need and are able to fully release your creative energies, you will become very successful. A great opportunity may come from a lowly source.

59. IMAGE: *buried treasure*

What you seek will be out of your reach unless obstacles are removed. Discover your inner strengths and talents or your growth will be limited, you will have trouble finding companionship, and there will be few to help you. Your sincerity will be challenged. Be circumspect to avoid troubles. If you cultivate your inner virtue, do what is just, and are willing to help others, good fortune will follow.

60. IMAGE: *a trespasser*

Be careful to keep disintegrative conditions from entering your life. Be on guard against saboteurs and do not entertain relations with destructive people. Be patient in the face of restrictions. You will invite great losses if you violate the boundaries of others. It is better to wait for positive signs. Help will come from high-minded persons. You will be fortunate if you bear a child.

61. IMAGE: *a pot of gold*

Your fortunes will flourish. Beware of becoming overly ambitious, however, or you will fall. Nothing and no one is entirely independent. Be humble and considerate of others and you will avoid pitfalls. Many opportunities for success will come your way. You will be helped by someone in a high place.

62. IMAGE: *a cloudless autumn sky*

Patiently bring things through to completion and you will reap a good harvest. Be gentle; relentless striving will meet with misfortune. Temper your ambition and strive to grow inwardly. Though success is yours, you must be humble. Be vigilant. Wait for the right time to advance.

63. IMAGE: *paradise*

You will attain whatever you wish for. The greater your effort, the greater your gain. Be firm of purpose. Cooperate with those above and below you. Success and prosperity will come to you through creative work, especially through writing. Spiritual work will progress unobstructedly.

64. IMAGE: *a fox*

Be careful that you aren't secretly on the defensive while seeking to join forces with others. Mistrusting others will cause them to mistrust you. Your insincerity will alienate others. Seek to balance your heart and mind. Blind passion will result in entanglement and losses. Clarify your aims. Vacillating and worrying accomplish nothing. Stay centered and you will become secure and prosperous.

EXERCISE

If your door fortune has negative content, you can disperse or break up its negative chi by hanging wind chimes near the doorway or hanging a string of bells from the door's hinges inside the door. They should ring whenever you open and close it.

By now you should have filled out your personal data list. In Part 2, you will see how all the information in your list applies to the arrangement of your home.

part two

BRINGING HARMONY
AND BALANCE
TO YOUR HOME

chapter 9

INTRODUCTION TO THE THREE DIAGNOSTIC METHODS

There are three methods we will use to diagnose the problematic conditions of your space. The first is called the "eight point method." The second involves reading the space according to the five elements. The third method superimposes a figure of a human body (a stick figure) over the floor plan.

The eight point method shows the relation of problematic areas in your space to the various concerns of your life, such as your career, finances, and relationships. The methods of reading the space according to the five elements and of superimposing a stick figure over the floor plan show the relation of the problematic areas in your space to your emotions and health.

THE EIGHT POINT METHOD

Although the eight point method is not as old as the purely classical methods used in feng shui, it has become popular among many practitioners. The eight point method is used for diagnosing and treating problems and for locating meaningful areas for the placement of furniture, objects of art, and plants. Each of the eight points, or areas, has a name. They are called the career point, the knowledge point, the family point, the money point, the reputation point, the marriage point, the children point, and the friends point (which includes communication and travel). When we put them on the map, they appear as shown in the diagram on the following page, figure 17.

(*fig. 17*)

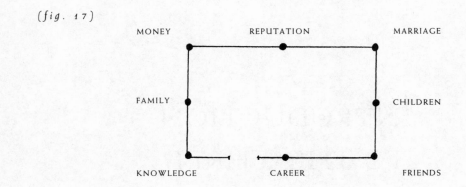

The line on which you find the points called friends, career, and knowledge always corresponds to the wall of the main doorway. To locate the points, or areas in the space, stand, or imagine that you are standing, in the doorway looking *in*.

To apply the diagram to your space, first superimpose it on the floor plan of your entire home, and then superimpose it on the floor plan of each room. If your space is a studio apartment, superimpose the diagram on the floor plan of the studio alone, and not on any imagined areas within it. If your home has an irregular shape, extend the lines of its contours until you get a square or rectangle, as shown in figure 18.

The eight point method is not always so easily applied. There are places that have such odd shapes that several of the points appear to be missing.

(*fig. 18*)

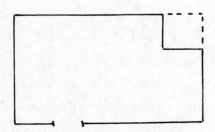

In a space of two or more rooms, in which the overall shape lacks more than one point, as shown in figure 19, look for the points in the separate rooms, as shown in figure 20. The overall space in figure 19 appears to be lacking both the money and the friends points. However, both the money and friends points can be found in both rooms.

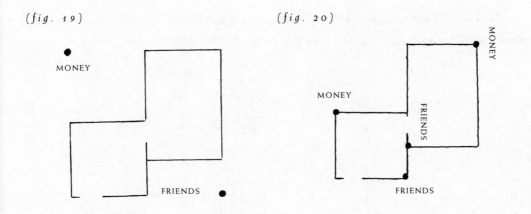

(fig. 19)   (fig. 20)

If your space seems to be impossible to understand by the eight point method, as suggested by figure 21, either reassign the points so that they take in as much of the space as possible, as shown in figure 22, or treat the space in the same manner as shown in figure 20.

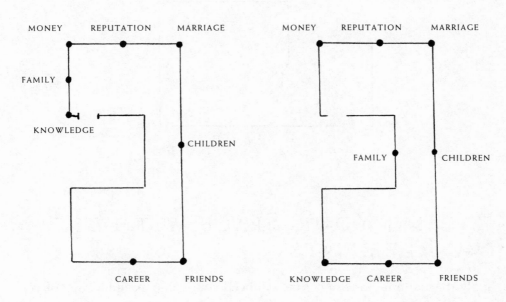

(fig. 21)   (fig. 22)

In a studio apartment that lacks one point, as in figure 23, you can create the point by using a screen to divide the room, as shown in figure 24.

(fig. 23)

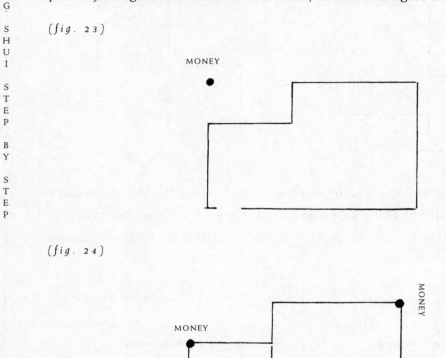

(fig. 24)

READING YOUR SPACE WITH THE FIVE ELEMENTS

To apply this important method, you will need your compass and a copy of your floor plan.

If the shape of your overall space is irregular, fill it out with a dotted line until you get a square or rectangle, as shown in figure 25. Once you have done that, draw diagonal lines from corner to corner, as shown in figure 26. The place where the diagonal lines cross is your siting point. Standing at that point, use your compass to find where north, northeast, east, and the rest of the directions lie in the space. Mark them on your floor plan, as shown in figure 27.

The next step is to write down the element of each of the directions, as shown in figure 28:

- Water for north
- Earth for northeast and southwest
- Wood for east and southeast
- Fire for south
- Metal for west and northwest.

(fig. 25)

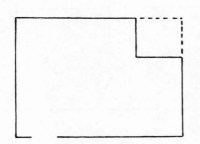

(fig. 26)

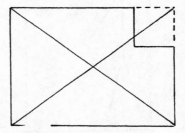

(fig. 27)

(fig. 28)

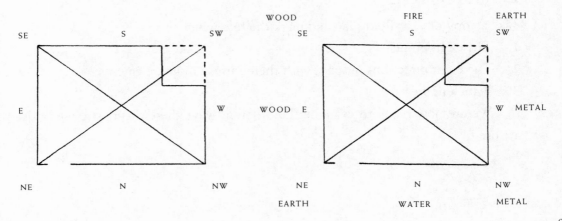

WORKING WITH A STICK FIGURE

To apply this diagnostic method, sketch a stick figure on your floor plan. Don't worry about your artistic ability. Draw its head at the main entrance and fill out the length of the space with the rest of the body, as shown in figure 29. If the entrance is in the middle, draw the body across the width of the space, as shown in figure 30.

(fig. 29)   *(fig. 30)*

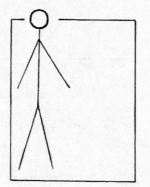

EXERCISE

Take a copy of your floor plan and mark the following:

1. The eight points.
2. The eight directions in space with their corresponding elements.
3. A stick figure.

    We are now ready to examine the different ways these diagnostic methods are used.

chapter 10

THE EFFECTS OF CLUTTER

Your home breathes like a living body. Its breath, or chi, comes in and out through the doors and windows and flows through the corridors and rooms. When it flows unobstructedly it imparts the sensations of ease and comfort. But when its flow is obstructed due to clutter, the opposite happens: your chi becomes obstructed, the elements in your body become unbalanced, and your health and affairs suffer.

In numerous feng shui consultations over the past several years, I have noticed certain common patterns involving clutter. Clutter is related to instincts of self-protection and hoarding, on the one hand, and to feelings of insecurity, on the other. Clutter corresponds essentially to the Earth element. If Earth is negative, you worry. Positive Earth nurtures. The person who clutters needs nurturing, or needs to be provided with nourishment and support. If you tend to clutter, you should ask yourself what you need to feel secure and happy, and what it is that you believe about yourself that prevents you from having it.

To draw an example of how clutter can relate to your emotions, I once worked on the apartment of a man who had been suffering from severe anxiety for years. His apartment was totally cluttered with papers, old boxes, and damaged furniture. Even though he knew how the clutter negatively affected him, the man felt unable to do anything about it.

Clutter near the doorway always indicates resistance to going out into the world. If you have doorway clutter, you have to struggle through a lot that seems to stand in the way of your goals. You tend to barricade yourself in and fear letting go. Cluttered shelves overhead, or things piled up to the ceiling indicate that you are apprehensive that something unwanted might befall you.

Clutter caused by things stored under your bed causes chi to stagnate and generates sha, which your body absorbs when you sleep. If you have things stored under your bed, even if they are neatly stored in boxes, remove them and store them somewhere else—your health will improve.

You can easily resolve clutter in closets by sorting out your things, discarding what is no longer useful, and organizing what is left in boxes, envelopes, or whatever is appropriate.

Now let's examine the effects of clutter using the three diagnostic methods.

CLUTTER AND THE EIGHT POINT METHOD

Clutter found at any of the eight points indicates unsettled or troubled conditions in the corresponding area of your life. If furniture or other large objects are arranged at any of the points in a way that feels or appears obstructive, it indicates obstacles in the corresponding area of your life that are holding you back. For instance, if there is a confused mass of objects at the marriage point of your bedroom, it would be safe to say that you are not too happy about what is developing in your marriage or in your love life. You might even be completely blocked. If you clear up the clutter and arrange something beautiful in its place, such as an intimate seating area, a table with a vase of flowers, or a large standing plant, you set harmonious thoughts in motion and attract love into your life.

Clutter at the children point indicates worry about children and/or creative projects.

Clutter at the friends point indicates that you are having trouble with communication and with creating friendships.

Clutter at the career point indicates that you are troubled about your career.

Clutter at the knowledge point indicates that you have difficulties gaining knowledge.

Clutter at the family point indicates confused family relations.

Clutter at the money point indicates that you are worried and confused about your finances.

Clutter at the reputation point indicates that you are troubled about your reputation.

CLUTTER AND THE FIVE ELEMENTS

Clutter found in the various directions of space affects the corresponding elements in your life as follows:

If clutter is found throughout your home, the element Earth is being affected. This indicates a tendency to worry too much about yourself and points to problems affecting the stomach, spleen, and pancreas.

If clutter occurs in the northeast and/or the southwest, it also affects the element Earth and produces the same effects.

If clutter is found in the west and/or the northwest, the element Metal is being affected. This reveals a tendency to be in conflict over issues of control. It also points to grief and to problems affecting the lungs and large intestine.

If clutter is found in the north, the element Water is being affected. This indicates a tendency to hide one's feelings from oneself and from others, and points to anxieties and to problems affecting the kidneys and bladder.

If clutter occurs in the east and/or southeast, the element Wood is being affected. This reveals a tendency to become confused and indecisive, and points to anger and to problems affecting the liver and gallbladder.

If clutter is found in the south, the element Fire is being affected. This indicates a tendency to become troubled over affairs of the heart and points to volatile moods, and to problems affecting the heart, the small intestine, the digestion, and the immune function.

WORKING WITH A STICK FIGURE

If you view the cluttered areas of your home in relation to your drawing of a stick figure, you can see where your body is being affected (see figure 31).

(*fig. 31*)

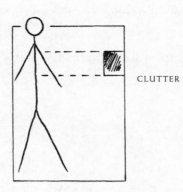

CLUTTER

LUCY

Readings using the stick figure method can be quite interesting. Some years ago I met a young woman, Lucy, who had been suffering from an undiagnosable illness ever since her husband's death three years earlier. Frustrated at the inability of her doctors to help her, Lucy asked me to come to her home, an artist's loft, to examine its condition. Walking through the space, I found the chi harmonious, with the exception of a huge pile of photographic equipment covered by a drop cloth positioned near the entrance (fig. 32).

(*fig. 32*)

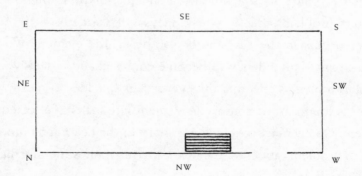

The photographic equipment had belonged to Lucy's husband. When I recommended that she remove it, she told me she didn't want to, that the photographic equipment reminded her of her husband and that she was not emotionally ready to let go of him. Still wishing to help Lucy, as she was really very ill, I recommended that she see a Chinese doctor with whom I was acquainted.

Some time later the doctor, having examined Lucy, called to say that he suspected there was a large cluttered mess near the entrance of her home and, if he was not mistaken, that I should tell her to get rid of it. I assured him that I had already spoken to Lucy and that she was unwilling to take action. The doctor, convinced there was a direct connection between the condition of her home and her health, discussed the matter with Lucy himself.

The stick body figure sketched in figure 33, with its head at the door, reveals more significant information about Lucy's condition at that time:

(*fig. 33*)

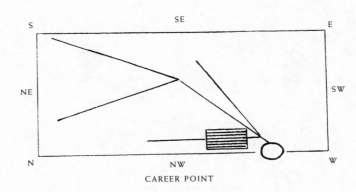

The pile of photographic equipment stood as a constant reminder to Lucy of her husband and became the symbol of her unresolved grief. She instinctively placed it where it would do her the most harm. In relation to her body, as represented by our drawing, it affected her lungs, heart, and the function called heart constrictor, which maintains feelings of love, protects the heart, and controls the immune function. Looking at the body in relation to its direction in space, the northwest, which corresponds to Metal, the pile indicates problems involving the lungs and large intestine. It also points to unresolved control issues; Lucy simply was not willing to let go of her grief. It is also significant that the pile of equipment was so close to the door, almost as though she were trying to barricade herself in.

In time, as she began to respond to the doctor's treatment and encouragement to follow my recommendation, Lucy sold the photographic equipment, and soon after recovered her health, quit her job, and moved away to the Southwest, where she had always wanted to live. Finally, she was free.

GWEN

Although it initially may seem complicated, all three methods (the eight point method, the five element method, and the stick figure method) can be easily combined. The result will give you a very clear picture of what's wrong and how to treat it. For example, let's look at the situation of Gwen, who was very lonely and having serious financial problems. Gwen lived in a studio apartment that was cluttered in three areas, as shown in figure 34.

With a sketch representing her body and the relevant compass directions and points, shown in figure 35, we can learn quite a few things.

(fig. 34)

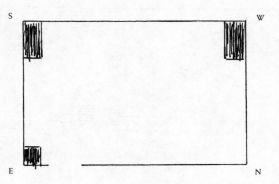

(fig. 35)

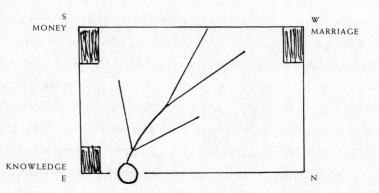

If we look at the sketch of the apartment in relation to the sketch of Gwen's body, the areas of clutter appear to affect her neck, or throat, and lower legs. The elements to which the throat and lower legs correspond are Wood and Metal, respectively, and as Metal destroys Wood, it reveals a conflict of the desires to control and to grow. It was difficult for Gwen to make plans and decisions.

Clutter in the east, south, and west areas involves the elements Wood, Fire, and Metal, showing tendencies toward being confused and indecisive, troubled over affairs of the heart, and in conflict over control issues. It also points in the east to anger and problems possibly involving the liver and gallbladder; in the south to volatile moods and problems possibly involving the heart, the small intestine, the digestion, and the immune function; and in the west to grief and problems possibly involving the lungs and large intestines.

If you look at the space according to the eight point method in combination with the five elements, you can see that, as Gwen's knowledge point was east, her ability to know and understand herself and her situation was weakened by her tendencies to be confused and indecisive. Moreover, as Gwen's money point was south, her financial growth was weakened by her tendencies to be troubled over affairs of the heart. Finally, since Gwen's marriage point was to the west, her need for a partner was inhibited because of difficult control issues.

The most effective way for her to resolve these problems required that she work inwardly at the same time she sorts out all the clutter. Thus Gwen worked at resolving her control issues while reorganizing the marriage point in the west and began to feel more hopeful about her prospects for love. Also, as Gwen became more resolved in her emotions and worked at reorganizing the money point in the south, she began to feel a greater sense of security and self-confidence, which led her to take positive steps to improve her finances. Finally, Gwen arrived at decisions she needed to make while reorganizing the knowledge point in the east. Many of her needs became clearly focused and she began to feel more adventurous.

EXERCISES

Analyze the clutter in your home. If you have more than one room, first view your space as a whole, and then view each of the rooms individually, using in both cases the three diagnostic methods. If your home is a studio, view it as a whole.

In which areas do you find clutter? Do you find parallel cluttered areas in your home as a whole and one or more of its rooms? For example, do you find the money point of the whole house as well as the money points of the living room, the bedroom, and the kitchen all cluttered?

Using the method of the five elements with the eight point method, what emotions do you find involved in the troubled areas?

Synthesize all the information you've obtained using the three diagnostic methods and determine what it says about you. How does it relate to what you learned about yourself in the first part of this book?

Sorting out the cluttered areas in your home, discard what is no longer useful and organize what is. If you do, your activities will take on new vitality.

Inauspicious Placements of Doors and Windows

When windows or doors are situated too close to the corners of a room the chi escapes too quickly. The exception to this is the main door to a house or the main door to a room. If you look at this problem using the eight point method, you can see how a window or passageway that is too close to a corner can cause the chi to rush out and produce the effect of a depletion or loss in the corresponding area of your life. The following cases will illustrate this problem.

Al

Al was living in a cramped apartment whose kitchen door had been removed:

(fig. 36)

In addition, there were no curtains or blinds on the kitchen window, which was mere inches from the corner of the room.

Al's Chinese horoscope and door fortune revealed to me that he was prosperous. However, the problems in his apartment indicated that he spent all of his money. He confirmed this to be true. Al had been unhappy with his cramped living conditions and wanted to move. The only problem was that, in his frustration, he had developed the self-defeating habit of overspending.

If you imagine the chi as a stream that enters through the main door and passes through the space, it will appear to be doing this:

(fig. 37)

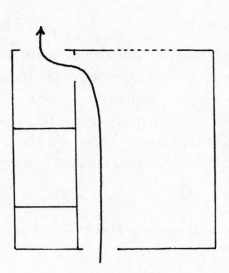

It escapes at the money point. The solution was quite simple; I recommended that Al put back the kitchen door and hang curtains on the kitchen window.

When Al decided to carry out these and other recommendations involving the removal of clutter and the use of color, his feelings of frustration abated, and he began to reorganize his finances and make plans to move to a larger, more comfortable apartment.

PAT AND TOD

Pat and Tod live in a house whose basic shape is like this:

(fig. 38)

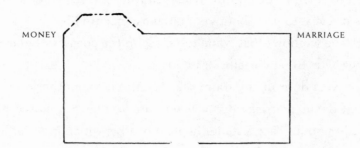

MONEY   MARRIAGE

At the money point, situated at the back end of the living room, there was a rather large bay window with French doors that opened out to a garden. At the marriage point there was an unused lavatory in which the plumbing was in serious disrepair. The lavatory was adjacent to a small, cluttered room that was once a maid's room and was now a storeroom, directly next to the kitchen.

The conditions at the money point and the marriage point revealed to me that Pat and Tod were in financial straits and their marriage was coming apart. They confirmed this to be true.

To help correct these undesirable conditions, I recommended that they hang lace curtains in the bay window at the money point, as the curtains would hold in the chi and therefore their money. At the marriage point, I suggested that they take out the lavatory, break down the bathroom wall, and create a special studio. The new space when uncluttered and enlarged would have the effect of opening the chi at the marriage point and easing the tensions in their marriage.

Soon after Pat and Tod had made these and other changes involving the use of colors, they began to feel happier and more secure. Both their finances and their relationship began to improve.

EXERCISES

Look through your entire home using the eight point method. Are there any areas where the chi rushes out due to inauspiciously placed windows or doorways? What does it reveal to you about your circumstances in life?

If you have windows that come too close to the corners of your rooms, cover the windows with either curtains or blinds.

If you have a door in any room that opens out to another room at either the money point or the marriage point, make sure you keep it closed to prevent the chi from rushing out. Place a standing plant nearby, which is either living or made of silk, to partially camouflage the door.

Windows and doors at the midpoints of the walls at the career, family, reputation, and children points are not a problem and need no special treatment.

chapter 12

LOOKING AT THE SHAPE OF YOUR SPACE

Now let's explore irregularities of architectural design using our three diagnostic methods and treatment for these problems using mirrors, plants, screens, and colors.

USING THE STICK FIGURE METHOD

If you view your space as a container, or envelope, for your body, you can see how the irregularities in its shape will tend to oppress your chi.

The shape in figure 39 appears to pinch the head and narrow the view; narrow-mindedness and/or headaches, literal and figurative, are implied. The space can be opened with the use of mirrors. Full-length mirrors can be placed on either or both walls, as indicated by the arrows in figure 40.

(fig. 39)   *(fig. 40)*

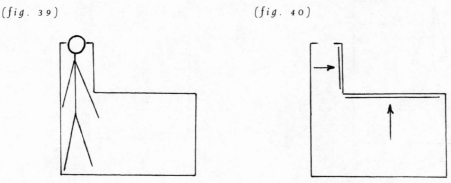

A second, less costly way is to take a copy of your floor plan and extend the lines until you have a square or rectangle. Then draw two crossing diagonal lines, as shown in figure 41. The points where the diagonal lines bisect the walls are the most critical, and they are precisely where you should hang mirrors, as indicated by the circles in figure 42.

(fig. 41)   *(fig. 42)*

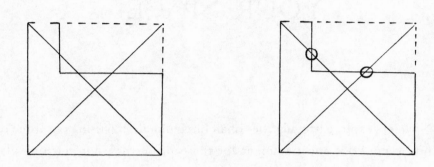

Figure 43 shows another irregular space oppressing the upper torso, or thorax, and therefore the heart, the lungs, and the heart constrictor function, which implies grief and troubled feelings of love.

If you were to mirror an entire wall, the best one would be the wall indicated by arrow A in figure 44. The next best would be that shown by arrow B.

(fig. 43)   *(fig. 44)*

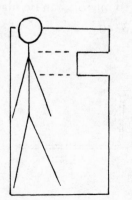

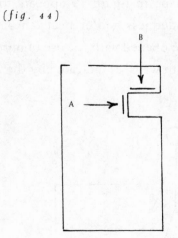

The space shown in figure 45 oppresses the middle of the torso, or upper abdomen, and therefore the liver, gallbladder, stomach, spleen, pancreas, and small intestine. This space implies anger, worry, digestive problems, and difficulty assimilating new ideas. Its treatment would be the same as that shown in figure 44.

The space shown in figure 46 oppresses the lower torso, or lower abdomen, and therefore the kidneys, bladder, sexual organs, and large intestine. The space implies fear and grief.

In addition to the indications listed above, all three of these shapes in figures 43 through 46 oppress the function called the triple heater, which regulates the digestive fires and the body heat in the upper, middle, and lower torso.

The space shown in figure 47 hinders movement, which makes it difficult to realize goals and causes frustration and anger. The way to treat this space is the same as shown in figures 40 through 42 above.

(fig. 45)   *(fig. 46)*   *(fig. 47)*

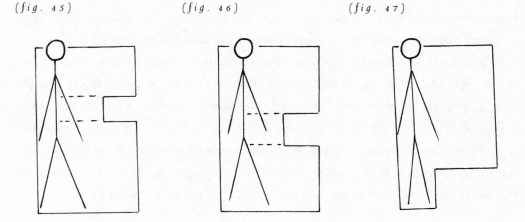

Although the L-shaped room is common, it is considered in feng shui to be unbalanced. You might apply mirrors to it, as shown in figures 40 through 42, or, if it is spacious enough, you can define its areas with standing plants, a screen, or a piece of furniture such as a couch or chest of drawers, as shown in figure 48.

(fig. 48)

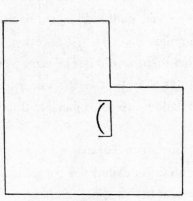

USING THE FIVE ELEMENT METHOD

I will now discuss an important technique that you can use to balance the energy of your space with colors, regardless of your birth star or lucky stars.

In order to demonstrate this technique, I have drawn figure 49 to serve as a basic reference model. Note that the corners of this model point to the northeast, southeast, southwest, and northwest. If the corners of your home don't point in these directions, but point to the cardinal directions—north, east, south, and west—the irregularities in the shape of your home will not exactly resemble those illustrated in figures 50 through 68. This, however, does not change any of the indications or remedies. Study this section carefully to find how it applies to your space.

(fig. 49)

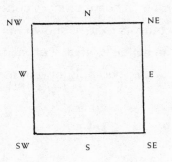

When a space is shaped irregularly, an element will correspondingly become exaggerated or depressed. If you carefully examine your floor plan, you will be able to tell an exaggerated or depressed area by its relative size to the main area of your space. The main area of the space is always larger than the exaggerated or depressed area. An exaggerated area protrudes from the main area like an annex and a depressed area indents the main area. Do not confuse the main area with an exaggerated or depressed area. An exaggerated or depressed area is never really more than one-third the size of the main area.

Exaggerated Areas

NORTH Where north is exaggerated, the element Water is out of balance and too strong. If Water tends to be out of balance in your body, and you live in a space such as this, your symptoms will become intensified. You could suffer from feelings of fear, of being overwhelmed or inundated by problems, or your emotions could become blocked. Symptoms of stress will also tend to show up in the nervous system, the bones and joints, or the kidneys, bladder, adrenals, and sexual organs. In relation to your activities, an exaggerated north will tend to attract difficult conditions for travel and business. It is also said to invite theft.

To remedy an exaggerated north area, as shown in figure 50, affix mirrors to the walls, as shown in figure 51:

(fig. 50) *(fig. 51)*

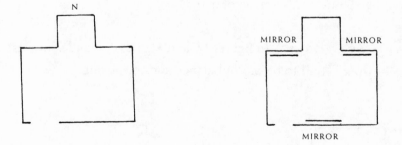

A second, more sophisticated remedy, involves painting and decorating the exaggerated north area, especially the north wall, in green and/or light blue. A very effective decoration here would be a blue vase with reeds. You might also consider hanging an upright, rectangular mirror with a green or blue wooden frame on the north wall.

NORTHEAST AND SOUTHWEST In figures 52, 53, and 54, the northeast and southwest are exaggerated, showing Earth to be out of balance and too strong.

(fig. 52)   (fig. 53)   (fig. 54)

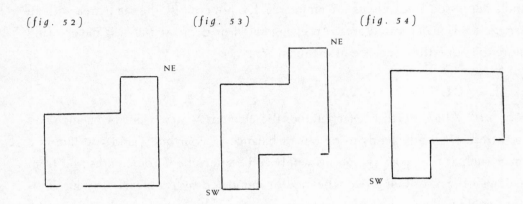

Too much Earth indicates selfishness, imperiousness, stubbornness, loss of equilibrium, obesity, abdominal swelling, and eating disorders. In addition to these indications, figure 52 shows prosperity that is ultimately lost because of greed; figure 53 shows losses due to covetousness and theft; and figure 54 shows a powerful and overbearing housewife and mother.

To remedy these, use white inside the expanded areas. You could also hang round or oval mirrors there, as indicated by the arrows. If the mirrors have frames, they should be white and/or made of metal.

EAST AND SOUTHEAST In figures 55 and 56, the east and southeast are exaggerated, showing Wood to be out of balance and too strong.

(fig. 55)   (fig. 56)

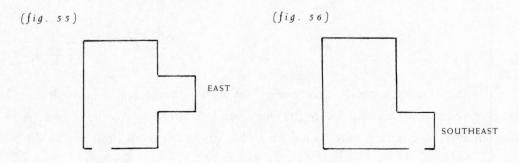

Too much Wood indicates excessive anger, distorted vision, both figurative and literal, as well as congested conditions of the liver and gallbladder.

To remedy these, paint and decorate the expanded areas in shades of red and/or purple, or you might put a red or purple vase with lots of brightly colored flowers there.

SOUTH In figure 57, the south is exaggerated. It shows Fire to be too strong and out of balance.

(fig. 57)

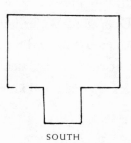

SOUTH

Too much Fire indicates volatile emotions, excessive striving, emotional and mental stress, as well as digestive troubles, high blood pressure, and heart disorders.

To remedy this space, color the expanded south area yellow or another earth tone. You can also hang a square mirror with a yellow or brown frame, and/or make a small indoor rock garden on the south wall to good effect.

WEST AND NORTHWEST In figures 58 and 59, the west and northwest are exaggerated, showing Metal to be out of balance and too strong.

(fig. 58)   *(fig. 59)*

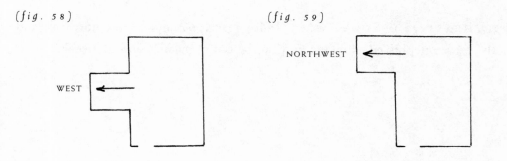

Too much Metal indicates extreme willfulness, grief, a blockage of the emotions, as well as troubles with the large intestines and lungs. In addition, excessive expansion in the west shows declining fortunes. Excessive expansion in the northwest shows an arrogant husband and father.

To remedy these problems, use black or midnight blue in the expanded areas. You can also hang round or oval mirrors with black frames on the walls indicated by the arrows.

INDENTED AREAS

NORTH In figure 60, the north is depressed, or indented, showing Water to be out of balance and too weak. Depressed Water indicates such conditions as low vitality, mental depression, obstructed flow of thought, poor adaptability and anxiety, as well as poor elimination, toxicity, sexual debilitation, dryness of joints, and illnesses affecting the ears, nerves, bladder, and kidneys.

(fig. 60)

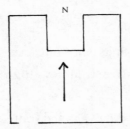

To remedy this spatial imbalance, hang something dark, with black or midnight blue, on the inner wall or, if you wish, paint the wall deep blue. You can also hang a round or oval mirror with a black frame on the wall pointed out by the arrow. If the mirror is tinted blue, so much the better.

NORTHEAST AND SOUTHWEST In figures 61, 62, and 63, the northeast and southwest are depressed, showing Earth to be out of balance and too weak.

(fig. 61) *(fig. 62)* *(fig. 63)*

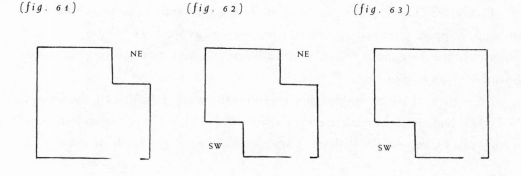

Depressed Earth conveys feelings of instability and of not being grounded and secure. It also points to disturbed sleep, poor nourishment, and problems with conception and childbearing. Figure 62 is the worst in this regard. In addition, figure 61 shows a need for protection, as it points to strange and unexpected happenings; figure 62 shows prosperity that does not last; and figure 63 shows a weak wife and mother.

To remedy these spaces, you can use yellow in the indented areas. In a space such as that in figure 62, you might put a yellow rug in the middle area. If space permits, you could also create small indoor rock gardens around the indented areas to compensate for the lack of Earth. If you wish to hang mirrors on the walls around the indented areas, they should be square and have yellow or brown frames.

EAST AND SOUTHEAST In figures 64 and 65, the east and southeast are depressed, showing Wood to be out of balance and too weak.

(fig. 64) *(fig. 65)*

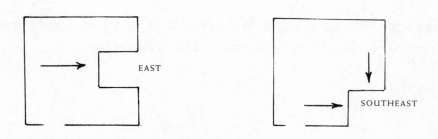

Depressed Wood indicates confusion, blocked thoughts and emotions, fears of being trapped, cramped, and smothered, as well as weakness of the limbs and illnesses of the liver and gallbladder. In addition, the depressed southeast is said to be unfortunate for business.

To remedy these conditions, use green on the walls indicated by the arrows. You could hang upright rectangular mirrors with green or blue wooden frames, as well as place standing plants there. They should be alive, not made of silk.

SOUTH In figure 66 the South is depressed, showing Fire to be out of balance and too weak.

(fig. 66)

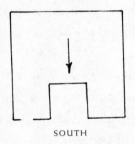

SOUTH

Depressed Fire indicates physical and emotional coldness, lack of receptivity, joylessness and difficulties in love, as well as poor eyesight, poor circulation, poor assimilation of food, coldness of the extremities, muscular tension, and speech impediments.

To remedy this space, use red or purple on the wall indicated by the arrow. The color doesn't have to be too intense; it could be a very subtle lavender, violet, or rose.

WEST AND NORTHWEST In figures 67 and 68, the west and northwest are depressed, showing Metal to be out of balance and too weak.

(fig. 67)   (fig. 68)

WEST

NORTHWEST

Depressed Metal indicates breakdowns of communication, emotional blocks and confused boundaries, as well as weaknesses affecting elimination and breathing.

To remedy these problems, use white on the walls around the indented areas. You can also place round or oval mirrors with white and/or metal frames in the places indicated by the arrows.

USING THE EIGHT POINT METHOD

View your space according to the eight point method and you will be able to see which areas of your life are being affected.

For example, if the career area is exaggerated, as in figure 57, your professional affairs will tend to become congested or overly complicated, and demand the lion's share of your time, keeping you away from home too much.

If the career area is depressed, as in figure 66, your professional affairs will tend to be hindered by untoward conditions, as well as by your own confusion and inability to move around obstacles.

If the knowledge area is exaggerated, as in figure 54, you might find your increased knowledge has led you to neglect other important areas of your life. You may also find out a bit late that much of what you learn is of little if any use to you.

If the knowledge area is depressed, as in figure 63, you will have to struggle against limitations to get information you need. A blind spot could develop in the way you understand your world.

If the family area is exaggerated, as in figure 58, family affairs will tend to become overly complicated and demand an inordinate amount of your time. This suggests an overbearing relative, possibly outside the nuclear family, who demands too much attention.

If the family area is depressed, as in figure 67, family life will be occasion for many cares. A family member may suffer from a long illness or other misfortune that will be of concern to you.

If the money area is exaggerated, as in figure 59, you will have big expenses and difficulties holding on to money, or will see your fortunes grow, only to become stagnant.

If the money area is depressed, as in figure 68, it will be difficult for you to develop your finances. You may also have to pay the expenses of someone else, only to be left short of funds in the end.

If the reputation area is exaggerated, as in figure 50, you might develop an extraordinary opinion of yourself while others discredit you. It may also be that many people will come to you asking for advice and help, only to deplete your chi.

If the reputation area is depressed, as in figure 60, you might very well find yourself keeping a low profile and living in obscurity. You might also develop the habit of living vicariously through someone else.

If the marriage area is exaggerated, as in figure 52, your marriage or love relationship may tend to become overly complicated and tense as you pull away from each other, even to the point of separation.

If the marriage area is depressed, as in figure 61, and you are alone, you may find it difficult to get involved with anyone, or, if you are involved, that many obstacles come up and intrude on your relationship.

If the children area is exaggerated, as in figure 55, and you have children, you may find them unruly and difficult to understand, or, if you don't have children, you might have a rather childish person in your life who demands too much of your attention.

If the children area is depressed, as in figure 64, conditions around the children will be rather unhappy and wanting in some important respect; you might not be willing to provide them with needed emotional comfort.

If the friends area is exaggerated, as in figure 56, your involvement with people outside may take you away from home; you could easily complicate your life by becoming involved in the affairs of others. You might also be traveling extensively at the expense of your home life since the friends point includes travel.

If the friends area is depressed, as in figure 65, friends could let you down. You might find it unnecessarily difficult to get help when you need it; it either does not come, or it comes too late. It will also be difficult to keep travel plans.

HARRY

Let me show you how our three diagnostic methods were used to diagnose and treat a space.

I was asked to look at Harry's apartment, the basic outline of which appears below in figure 69. Harry was suffering from ulcers and a nervous condition, which show up in the space by the indented areas pinching the middle of the stick figure and by the depressed northeast and southwest that correspond to the element Earth. Harry was a very lonely man. He apparently was unable to form an intimate relationship with anyone, shown by the depressed marriage area. He also seemed to be extremely opinionated, shown by the depressed knowledge area. Harry's problems with knowledge and marriage had a connection to the element Earth in that he worried excessively and felt insecure and ungrounded.

What I recommended he do to adjust the chi of the space was to place mirrors on the walls, as shown in figure 70, and put a yellow rug on the floor in the middle of his apartment, between the two indented areas.

(fig. 69)   (fig. 70)

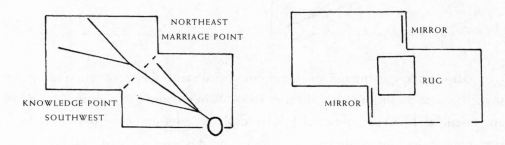

While seeking treatment for his poor health, Harry arranged his apartment as I had suggested. The chi became calm and bright, and because it gave him the sense of safety and security he needed, his nervousness abated, his health began to improve, and he began to cultivate a more positive outlook on life.

JOAN

Joan, on the other hand, was having financial difficulties and lived in the apartment whose basic outline appears in figure 71. In addition to Joan's financial problems, she suffered from lower back pain, as shown by the indented area. The exaggerated area also shows impeded progress in life—as her legs appear to be stuck there. The depressed marriage area in the west shows that her difficulties in finding a relationship involved emotional blocks and a breakdown of communication, while the exaggerated money area in the south shows that her financial problems were related to her emotional upsets in the past.

To remedy this, I recommended that Joan keep the indented walls in the marriage area white and hang round or oval mirrors on them. I also recommended that she use yellow and mirror the inside wall in the money area, as shown in figure 72.

(fig. 71)   *(fig. 72)*

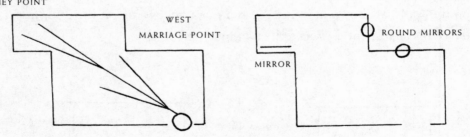

SOUTH
MONEY POINT

WEST
MARRIAGE POINT

ROUND MIRRORS

MIRROR

Joan's space was the mirror of her emotional state, therefore working on the space became an inspiration for inner work. While completely reorganizing her apartment, as I had recommended, Joan resolved to let go of the past, look for a better and more interesting job, and take renewed interest in her social life.

ANNE

Another woman, Anne, was distressed over her difficulties with various members of her family. The basic outline of her apartment appears in figure 73.

Anne tended to worry a lot, as shown by the indented area affecting the region of her stomach. The depressed family area in the northwest shows how troubled she was by broken communication with family members.

To remedy Anne's difficulties, I recommended that she use white around the indented area and, since it was not possible to hang a mirror on the more critical northwest wall, that she at least mirror the wall, as shown in figure 74.

Once Anne became aware of the subtle connection between the condition of her apartment and her difficulties, she decided to take the initiative simultaneously to rearrange her apartment and restore the communication with her relatives, with whom she so much wanted to be at peace.

(*fig.* 73)

(*fig.* 74)

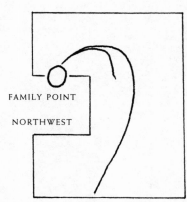

FAMILY POINT

NORTHWEST

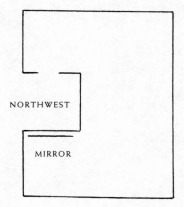

NORTHWEST

MIRROR

EXERCISES

1. Using our three diagnostic methods, analyze your own home, first as a whole, then looking at each room individually. Are there any irregularities of shape? If you draw a head at the door and fill out the whole space with a reasonably well-proportioned body, where do the irregularities of shape affect you? In which compass directions do you find them? Which of the eight points do they affect? Try to synthesize the information you get from the compass directions and their corresponding elements with the eight points. What do these say about your circumstances? How do these relate to what you found out about yourself in chapter 10?

2. Study the treatments for the different problems discussed in this chapter. Choose those that relate to the problems you find in your own space.

chapter 13

LOOKING AT EXTREMELY IRREGULAR SPACES

So far, we have discussed spaces that, though they may have irregularities, are designed on a single grid.

Now let's look at some homes that are designed on multiple grids superimposed at odd angles to one another. These homes give the feeling of floating and tension at one and the same time. Walls do not run parallel to one another, corners are not square, and rooms have unusual shapes. Curious things happen to the psychic energy, health, and fortunes of people who live in such places.

Because there are a seemingly infinite variety of these shapes, and because they all appear to be so plastic, the feng shui methods for diagnosing and treating them have to be correspondingly flexible; the approach has to be spontaneous and inventive.

In feng shui practice there are two basic shapes by which all irregularities are brought into balance: the circle, which symbolizes heaven, and the square, which symbolizes earth. All homes designed according to a single grid, such as those discussed in chapter 12, can be resolved to the square, or to its variant the rectangle. The circle can be effectively used for an unusually shaped home, especially if it is situated in the countryside, where it is possible to do landscaping that integrates and balances the shape of the home.

CHLOE

Figure 75 shows Chloe's apartment:

(fig. 75)

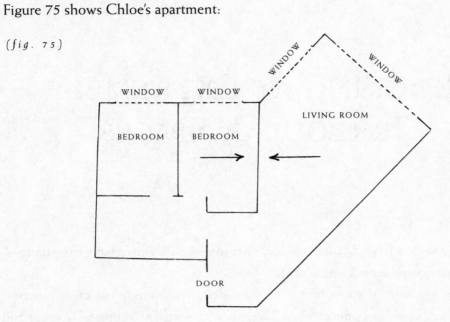

Can you see how her apartment is formed out of two overlapping grids? The riddle here was how to harmonize the two areas. This is how it was handled:

(fig. 76)

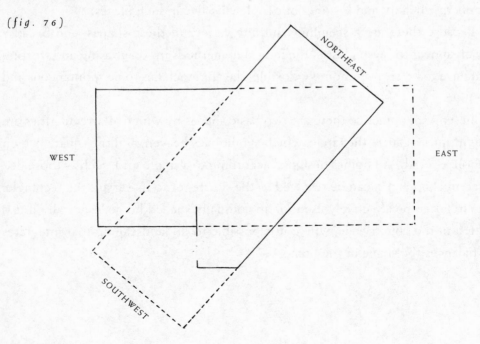

I ascertained that the elements of the rectangle running east and west were Wood and Metal, respectively, and the element of the rectangle running northeast and southwest was Earth. To integrate Wood, Earth, and Metal, we need Fire, as Wood generates Fire, Fire generates Earth, and so on. I therefore recommended that the wall, indicated by the arrows in figure 75, be painted a shade of red or purple.

I also recommended that a mirror be placed on the red wall in the living room to create the illusion of symmetry in an otherwise unbalanced shape.

LARRY AND RUTH

Figure 77 shows the plan of another unusual apartment whose shape caused its occupants, Larry and Ruth, to be in conflict with each other.

(fig. 77)

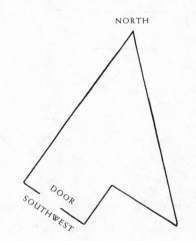

NORTH

DOOR
SOUTHWEST

This shape is basically a triangle, corresponding to Fire. The triangle is the most wrathful shape, inspiring expansiveness and aggression. In this apartment the apex aims due north, the direction of the element Water, and, with the doorway facing southwest, the apartment is ruled by the element Earth. Thus Fire and Earth are both out of harmony with Water and must be integrated.

Because the element Fire of the apartment's shape generates the element Earth that rules the apartment, and because the element Earth destroys the element Water, the apex does not merely aim at the north, it *attacks* the north.

What I did to pacify the energy was use the Earth of the doorway to support the Water in the north by affixing a small round mirror, corresponding to the element Metal, directly inside the apex to the north. Going one step further, I recommended that some plants be put in the area of the north point to draw the Water element harmoniously into the space. Thus, what was at first an outrageously warlike place was transformed into one of peace and harmony that allowed Larry and Ruth to relax and settle their differences.

LOUISE AND ALEX

Figure 78 shows an unusual house in the country I once worked on.

(fig. 78)

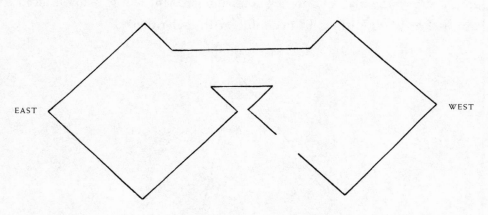

EAST   WEST

My first impression of this house was of a broken neck. The central part between the two squares is the kitchen. One square is to the east, or the direction of Wood, and the other square is to the west, or the direction of Metal. Metal cuts Wood; one half fights the other. The occupants of this house, Louise and Alex, were a married couple. When we were in the kitchen discussing what colors to use, they immediately began to argue with each another. Small wonder.

The colors I recommended for the kitchen, the area of greatest tension, were red and yellow, as their corresponding elements, Fire and Earth, create harmony between the Wood and Metal areas—Wood generates Fire (red), Fire generates Earth (yellow), and Earth generates Metal.

Once the opposition of the Wood and Metal areas was harmonized, it was necessary to figure out how best to integrate the entire structure. I decided to

work with the circle.

As shown in figure 79, the plan of the house was drawn with a circle around it. Then the lines from the four sides of the two squares were projected until they intersected the circumference.

At the places on the land corresponding to the points where the extended lines from the western square meet the circumference of the circle, I recommended that they install small rock gardens with red and purple flowers, and at the places where the extended lines from the eastern square meet the circumference of the circle, that they plant trees of one species, such as ash or alder.

(*fig. 79*)

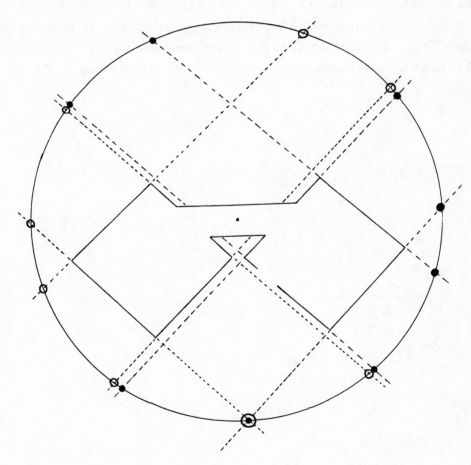

The circular pattern integrates the house in two ways: the first resolves the two conflicting squares into the circle of heavenly blessings, and the second creates another elemental bridge between Wood and Metal, consisting of the eastern square and the selected trees for Wood, the red and purple flowers for Fire, the rock gardens for Earth, and the western square for Metal.

EXERCISES

If you live in an unusual space, experiment with its floor plan until you discover its component forms; the plan will probably resolve into two or three rectangles. Using your compass, find out its directions, and according to its compass directions, find out its elements. Judge the harmony or discord of its elements according to the sequence of generation. What element is needed to make the necessary harmony? What color corresponds to the needed element? Try placing the needed color where the overlapping shapes join, as demonstrated in figures 75 and 76 above.

HARMONIZING THE CHI OF YOUR HOME WITH COLORS

You have already learned what your personal colors are from your birth and lucky stars and how to harmonize the element of your birth star with the element of your door's compass direction. You have also seen how colors can be used to balance irregularities of shape.

I will now show you how to use colors to bring each area within your home into complete harmony with the element of the door's compass direction, regardless of who lives in the house.

Take a copy of your basic floor plan. If you live in a house with two or more floors, you will need to work with the floor plan of each floor. Mark the door's compass direction. Remember, the door's direction is that which you face when looking directly out. Correspondingly, the direction of the second floor is that which you face when standing at the top of the stairs, looking down, and the direction of the basement is that which you face when standing at the bottom of the stairs, looking up. This method can also be applied to individual rooms, marking the door's direction, in each case, by facing out the door of the room.

You will have already projected the outlines of your space to get a square or rectangle, marked in the eight compass directions around the drawing, penciling in the two diagonal lines from corner to corner, as shown in figure 80, and drawing a radial diagram over the space to contain the eight compass areas, as shown in figure 81.

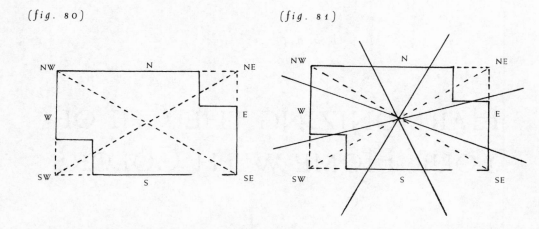

(fig. 80)   *(fig. 81)*

If your doorway faces south, the areas to the southwest, west, northwest, and northeast are out of harmony and in need of balancing. As shown in figure 82, use white in the areas to the southwest and northeast, and yellow in the areas to the west and northwest. White, as a range of color, includes ivory, gray, and silver; yellow includes everything from deep browns through tans and oranges to the lightest gold.

(fig. 82)

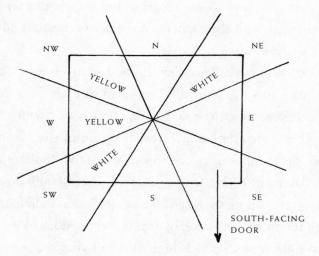

SOUTH-FACING
DOOR

The areas to the north, east, southeast, and south are all positive, and in no need of special treatment. You may use the color of your birth star, the color that harmonizes your birth star with the star of the doorway, or the colors of your lucky stars in these areas, if you wish.

If your doorway faces southwest, the areas to the north, east, southeast, and south are out of harmony and in need of balancing. As shown in figure 83, use white in the areas to the north and south, and red or purple in the areas to the east and southeast. Red and purple as a range of color include every hue from deep to light, and include such colors as rose, violet, and lavender.

(*fig. 8 3*)

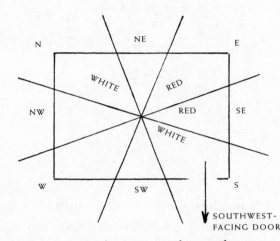

SOUTHWEST-
FACING DOOR

If your doorway faces west, the areas to the north, east, southeast, and south are out of harmony and in need of balancing. As shown in figure 84, use any hue of green and/or the lighter shades of blue in the area to the north; black, navy, or midnight blue in the areas to the east and southeast; and yellow in the area to the south.

(*fig. 8 4*)

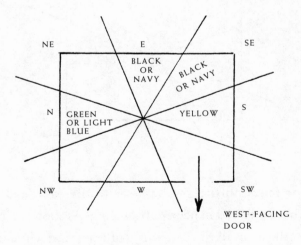

WEST-FACING
DOOR

If your doorway faces northwest, the areas to the north, east, southeast, and south are in need of balancing. As shown in figure 85, use green and/or light blue 131 in the areas to the north; black, navy, or midnight blue in the areas to the east and southeast; and yellow in the area to the south.

(fig. 85)

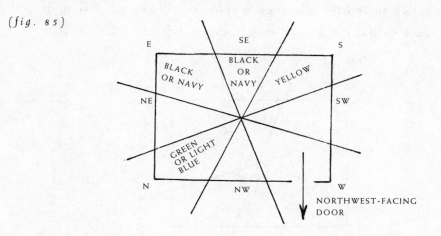

NORTHWEST-FACING DOOR

If your door faces north, the areas to the northeast, southwest, west, and northwest are out of harmony and in need of balancing. As shown in figure 86, use white in the areas to the northeast and southwest, and green and/or light blue in the areas to the west and northwest.

(fig. 86)

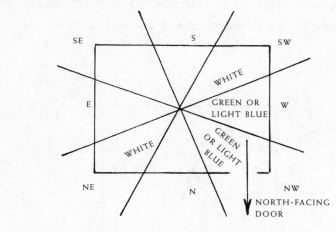

NORTH-FACING DOOR

If your door faces northeast, the areas to the east, southeast, south, and north are out of harmony and in need of balancing. As shown in figure 87, use reds and/or purples in the areas to the east and southeast, and white in the areas to the south and north.

(fig. 87)

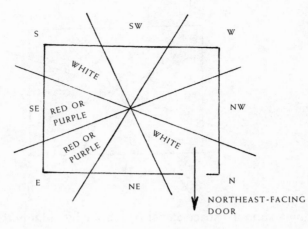

NORTHEAST-FACING
DOOR

If your door faces east, the areas to the southwest, west, northwest, and northeast are out of harmony and in need of balancing. As shown in figure 88, use reds and/or purples in the areas to the southwest and northeast, and black, navy, or midnight blue in the areas to the west and northwest.

(fig. 88)

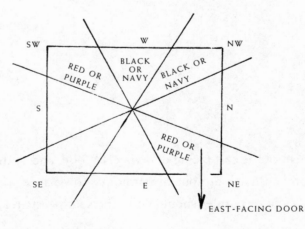

EAST-FACING DOOR

If your door faces southeast, the areas to the southwest, west, northwest, and northeast are in need of balancing. As shown in figure 89, use reds and/or purples in the areas to the southwest and northeast, and black, navy, or midnight blue in the areas to the west and northwest.

(fig. 89)

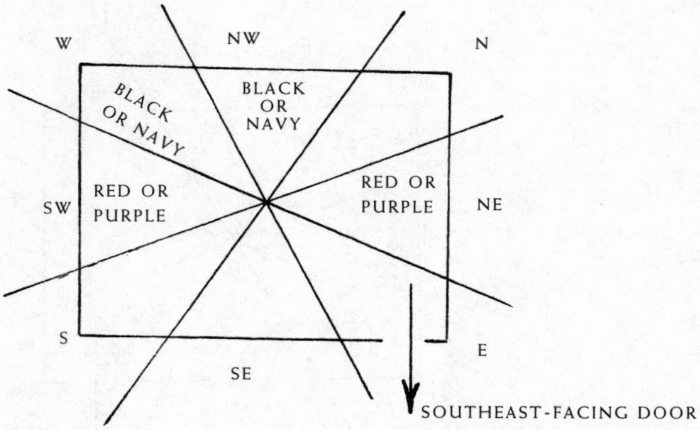

SOUTHEAST-FACING DOOR

Balancing an unusual space can also be done by judging the relationships of the different areas to the main doorway, in a different way. As in figure 90, first notice the element of the doorway, and then that of the area off the axis of the door.

(fig. 90)

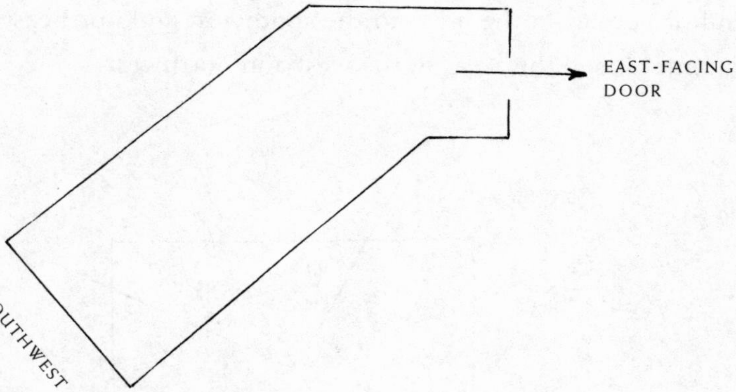

EAST-FACING DOOR

SOUTHWEST

The element of the east facing doorway is Wood, and of the southwest area it is Earth. Wood and Earth are out of harmony. To balance them, you need Fire. Therefore, reds and/or purples should go in the southwest area.

HUES OF YIN AND YANG

The last, but not least important detail to consider when deciding upon your use of colors is the hue, or level of darkness and brightness, according to yin and yang

aspects.

The choice of hue depends on two things: whether you want your home to be yin or yang to accommodate your physical makeup and occupation, and whether the relative function of a room is yin or yang.

The yang rooms are the living room, the kitchen, the dining room, the family room, the playroom or game room, and the home office. The yin rooms are the bedroom and the bathroom. The study and the studio apartment are both yin and yang. Thus, Fire colors in a living room would be different from Fire colors in a bedroom. In the living room they would be the brighter hues of reds and purples, while in the bedroom they would be the darker or more subtle shades of reds, plums, blue purples, lavender, and violet.

You are now ready to combine all three levels of our color system. Once you have determined the colors to balance your birth star with the door, to balance the irregularities of the shape of your space, and to bring each area in your space into harmony with the door, you will notice that there are areas in your space that don't require any special use of color. These are the areas where you can freely use your personal colors, as determined by your birth and lucky stars. You can also use your personal colors in the other areas in combination with the colors that are being used to harmonize the space. The following examples will show you how it is done.

ROSE

Rose, born on December 1, 1959, lives in the apartment illustrated in figure 91.

(fig. 91)

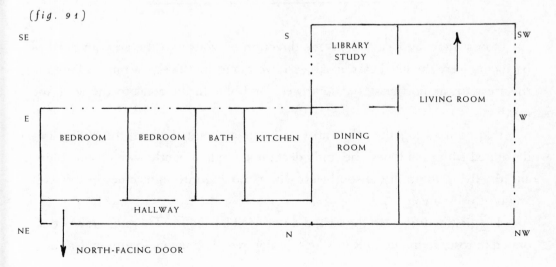

Rose's birth star is 1 Water Star, whose colors are black, navy, and midnight blue.

Since her doorway faces north, or Water, there is no disharmony between her door and her birth star.

Since Rose was born in the tenth Chinese solar month of a 1 Water Year, her lucky stars are 6 Metal and 7 Metal, whose colors are white and red, respectively. Combining these with the colors of her birth star, I had a basic palette of black and/or midnight blue, white, and red to work with.

To balance the irregularity of the shape of Rose's apartment, white was used in the exaggerated southwest area, and a round mirror was placed on the wall indicated by the arrow in figure 91.

To balance the different areas in the space that were out of harmony with the doorway, I first determined the middle of the apartment, as shown in figure 92, and delineated the eight areas, as shown in figure 93.

(fig. 92)

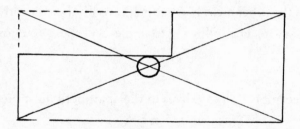

Rose's doorway faces north, the direction of Water, so the areas in need of balancing were the northeast, northwest, west, and southwest. White was used in the areas to the northeast and southwest, and blue in the areas to the west and northwest.

Putting it all together, the entire hallway was painted white, the dining area decorated with light blues, the study decorated predominantly with cream colors, and the living room in the southwest white, moving into light blues in the west and northwest areas.

The first bedroom, to the east, did not need balancing. Therefore it was decorated in rose, a yin hue of Rose's lucky color, red. The second bedroom was decorated in combinations of cream and rose. The bathroom was decorated in white and black. The kitchen was in the middle area, corresponding to the element Earth, and was out of harmony with the Water of the north-facing doorway. Thus, the kitchen was brought into balance by using all white, the color of Metal.

(fig. 93)

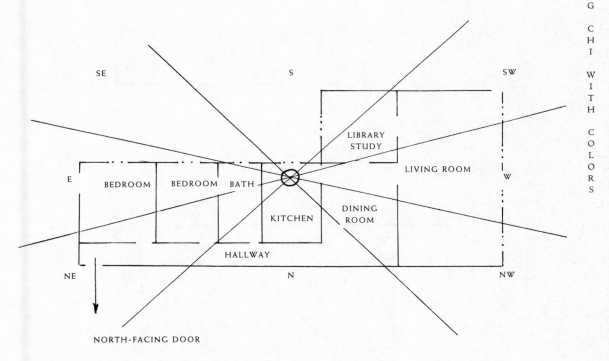

CHARLES

Now let's look at the apartment of Charles (fig. 94), whose birth star is 3 Wood and lucky stars are 1 Water and 9 Fire, giving him green, blue, white, and purple for his personal colors.

The conflict between the element of the doorway, Metal, and the element of Charles's birth star, Wood, was mitigated by painting the inside panel of the door black. This color not only resolved the conflict, but produced an elegant effect.

Delineating the different compass directions in the space, as shown in figure 95, I found that the areas to the north, east, southeast, and south were out of harmony and needed green, midnight blue, and yellow, respectively, to be balanced.

(*fig. 94*)

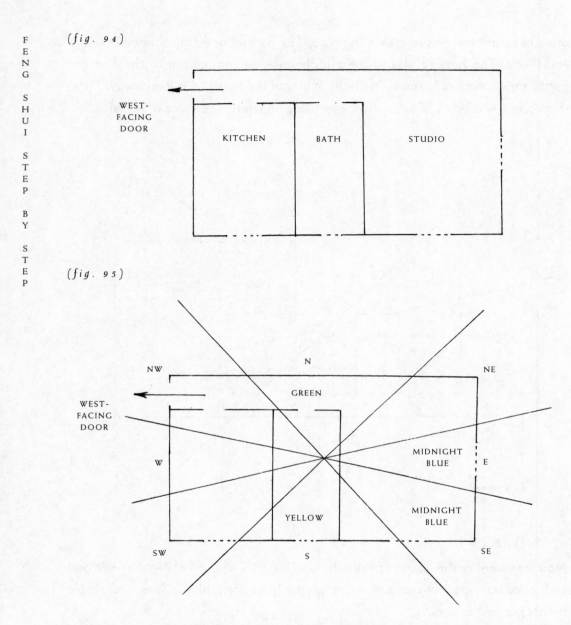

(*fig. 95*)

Thus, a green wall hanging was placed at the north point, the bathroom was decorated in white and gold, and the studio was painted white and decorated with a dark blue Chinese rug, a black-and-white African batik throw on the couch in the southeast corner, and black-and-white photographs on the walls, etc. Blue venetian blinds were also hung on the windows to bring blue light into the room and give it a cool, refreshing, and relaxed atmosphere.

RICHARD AND DOROTHY

Finally, let's look at the home of Richard and Dorothy, born March 22, 1959, and August 1, 1964, respectively:

(*fig. 96*)

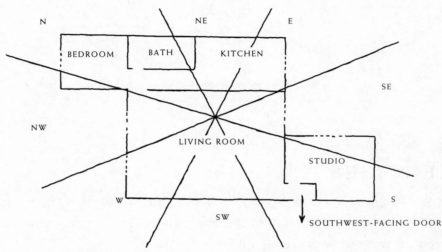

The birth dates gave 5 Earth and 6 Metal for their birth stars; 6 and 7 Metal for his lucky stars; and 2 Earth, 7 Metal, and 8 Earth for her lucky stars. 7 Metal is lucky for them both.

The color palette these stars yielded was yellow and white for 5 Earth and 6 Metal, and the lucky star colors black, red, and white for 2 Earth, 7 Metal, and 8 Earth. Red is lucky for them both.

As there was no conflict between either of the couple's birth stars and the doorway, nothing special was needed.

The exaggerated north and south areas of Richard and Dorothy's home needed to be balanced with colors. The north area needed light blue. The south area needed yellow.

Delineating the different compass directions in the space, as shown in figure 97, I found that the areas to the north, south, east, and southeast were out of harmony and needed white and red for balance.

Thus the bedroom was decorated in white and blues, the studio in white, tan, and red, the bathroom entirely in white, and red curtains were hung on the southeast-facing windows.

(fig. 97)

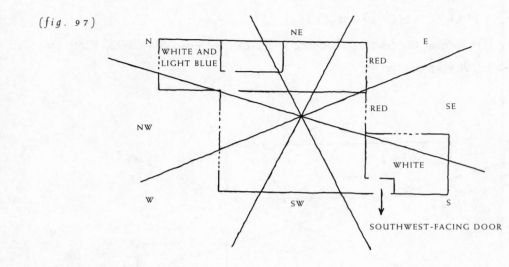

EXERCISES

Before you be gin applying colors to your home, either by painting, by using fabrics, or by the placement of pictures and other works of art, work out your entire color scheme on your floor plan as follows:

1. According to the method of the five elements described in chapter 12, select the colors you need to balance any exaggerated or indented areas.

2. According to figures 82 through 89, select the colors you need to balance the areas of your home with the compass direction of the main doorway.

3. Use the personal colors from your list of personal data, especially your lucky colors, in the areas of your home that don't need special colors for balancing. You may also combine your personal colors with the colors you are using for the areas that need balancing.

4. Tune the hues of your colors to yin or yang to suit your physical makeup, your occupation, and the relative functions of the different rooms, or areas, of your home. (See chapters 17 through 21 for in-depth descriptions of the different rooms and areas of your home.)

5. If you want to go into finer detail, you may apply the above steps to the individual rooms, in addition to the whole space. However, be aware of the activity the colors generate. If you're in a room that has too many colors, you will find it distracting.

6. Wait until you read the next few chapters before beginning to paint.

chapter 15

LIGHTING AND MIRRORS

⊘LIGHTING

Lighting is another element that can be used to balance the yin or yang of a room. Yang rooms should have brighter and more suffused lighting. Yin rooms, on the other hand, should have more intimate and localized lighting, with the possible exception of the bathroom.

If the front door opens to a small foyer, the foyer should be painted in a light hue and have soft lighting. Light hues create the illusion of more space. Intense hues, on the other hand, create the illusion of less space.

Stairways should always be well lit, and hallways, like veins and arteries that are both yin and yang, may be effectively lit by wall sconces placed at regular intervals.

MIRRORS

Mirrors are used for several reasons. They can create the illusion of depth, create symmetry in an otherwise unbalanced space, draw in pleasant views, magnify positive chi, activate stagnant chi, deflect attention, and repel sha.

You can create the illusion of depth with mirrors to remedy an irregular shape, as shown in figure 98.

To create symmetry in an unbalanced space, put a mirror on the slanted wall, as shown in figure 99.

(fig. 98)   *(fig. 99)*

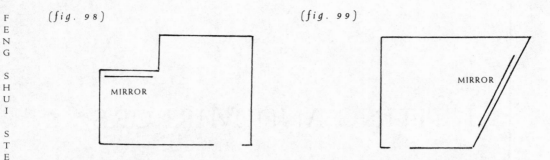

Pleasant views, such as bodies of water, mountains, trees, or gardens, stimulate beneficial chi. You can easily draw the views into a room so that they become visible from a chosen sitting point, such as a favorite chair, by finding the right spot on the wall to hang a mirror.

Magnifying positive chi is a method you can use to bring healing energy into a room. It is done with two mirrors of the same size. Depending on the door's compass direction, the healing point will be found in one of four relative positions in the room, as shown in figures 100 through 103.

(fig. 100)   *(fig. 101)*

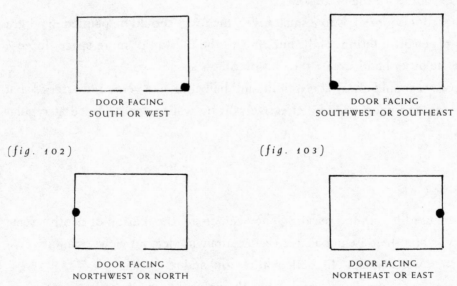

(fig. 102)   *(fig. 103)*

If the door faces south or west, the healing point in the room is located as shown in figure 100. If the door faces southwest or southeast, the healing point is located as shown in figure 101. If the door faces northwest or north, the healing point is located as shown in figure 102. If the door faces northeast or east, the healing point is located as shown in figure 103.

To do this correctly, place a crystal or some spiritual object such as a sacred book, symbol, or icon at the healing point and place mirrors on the two opposite walls of the room, as shown in figures 104 through 107.

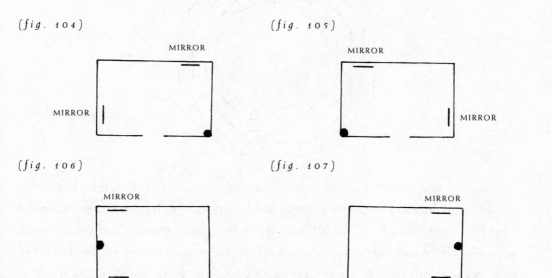

(fig. 104)   *(fig. 105)*

(fig. 106)   *(fig. 107)*

To activate stagnant chi, place a mirror in the stagnant area, such as an alcove or an area that receives too little light and/or circulation of air.

A mirror can be used to deflect attention as demonstrated in figure 108, showing a bedroom at the end of a hallway. The wall, indicated by the arrow, was constructed and fully mirrored to serve as a barrier and camouflage to the entrance. The position of the door was deliberately changed to create more privacy.

(fig. 108)

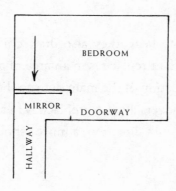

Small, round mirrors, such as the *ba gua* mirror shown in figure 109, can be used to repel sha.

(fig. 109)

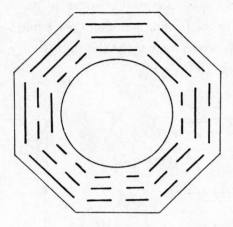

The ba gua mirror is a traditional feng shui instrument that can be bought in almost any Chinese bookstore or household supply store. It is an octagonal board with the eight trigrams of the *I Ching* painted in gold against a red background, with a small, round mirror in the center. It is meant to be hung or positioned to face and ward off the effects of secret arrows such as those listed in chapter 2. It can be hung outside the door or, if inside, directly in line with, and facing, the door. It can also be hung outside a window or placed on a windowsill. The secret to its efficacy lies not in its design, but in your intention. You can use any small, round mirror as a substitute for a ba gua mirror. If you position it believing it will effectively ward off sha, it will.

HANGING A MIRROR OVER A FIREPLACE

Although fireplaces generate heat, they also draw chi out of the room. Mirrors activate and intensify chi. If a fireplace is in an area of a room that is in a positive relation to the compass direction of the main door to the room, a mirror should be hung above the mantle. Conversely, if a fireplace is in an area of a room that is in a negative relation to the door's direction, a mirror should not be hung above the mantle.

Locating the compass directions in the room, if the door faces **north,** the positive areas are to the east, southeast, and south, and the negative areas are to the northeast, southwest, west, and northwest.

If the door faces **northeast,** the positive areas are to the southwest, west, and northwest, and the negative areas are the east, southeast, south, and north.

If the door faces **east,** the positive areas are to the north, southeast, and south, and the negative areas are to the southwest, west, northwest, and northeast.

If the door faces **southeast,** the positive areas are to the north, east, and south, and the negative areas are to the southwest, west, northwest, and northeast.

If the door faces **south,** the positive areas are to the north, east, and southeast, and the negative areas are to the southwest, west, northwest, and northeast.

If the door faces **southwest,** the positive areas are to the west, northwest, and northeast, and the negative areas are to the north, east, southeast, and south.

If the door faces **west,** the positive areas are to the southwest, northwest, and northeast, and the negative areas are to the north, east, southeast, and south.

If the door faces **northwest,** the positive areas are to the southwest, west, and northeast, and the negative areas are to the north, east, southeast, and south.

EXERCISE

Looking through your home and then at your floor plan, do you find any areas where you can use mirrors to balance the shape, activate the chi, repel secret arrows, and/or draw in pleasant views? Take note of them, but wait until after you have read chapters 16 through 21 before installing your mirrors.

chapter 16

FURNITURE AND DECOR

You are now ready to begin arranging your furniture. Before discussing the individual rooms in detail, however, let's look at your space as a whole and at the most comprehensive guidelines for arranging furniture and planning decor.

Imagine the chi as a stream that enters through the main door, flows everywhere throughout your home, and flows out and back in through the windows.

The chi is influenced by how you arrange your furniture and objects. The way you arrange, or position, them serves to guide, or conduct, the chi around and through the rooms and different areas of your home.

The chi should be made to flow smoothly and calmly throughout your home; it should neither rush nor stagnate in any one spot. The furniture and objects should be arranged in a comfortable, coordinated, and well-balanced manner.

The chi, ideally, should be made to circulate around the middle of your home as well as around the middle of each room. Imagine that the middle of your home is like the hub of a wheel. It should be left open. If you fill or clutter this area, you effectively suffocate the chi of your home. The middle of each room should also be left open, with the exception of the dining room and, possibly, the bedroom. The dining table should be at the center of the dining room. Unless the bedroom is very large, the bed will extend into the middle of the room.

The furniture generally should be positioned parallel to the walls. This creates the feeling of agreement and simplicity. If a room is large enough, however, you can also position pieces of furniture diagonally, in the corners, to create the feeling of roundness.

Avoid creating obstacles by awkward placements, by putting too much furniture in a room, or by using furniture that is too large for the space. A room that is overly furnished will force you to become sedentary and will lead to feelings of frustration.

Avoid blocking passageways, doors, or windows.

Do not block off or isolate any room. An isolated room, or area, causes chi to stagnate.

Avoid arranging furniture in a bow configuration in front of a door, as shown in figure 110, because it sends secret arrows, or sha, into the next room.

(fig. 110)

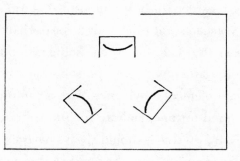

The key to the arrangement of a room is in the position of the most important piece of furniture (the bed in the bedroom, the desk in the study, your favorite sofa in the living room). Once you have found where the most important piece of furniture goes, arrange everything else in relation to it.

The walls of the rooms are protective barriers. Couches and chairs for the most part should have their backs to walls. If you sit with your back to a window or door, you will feel less secure than if you sit with your back to a wall. If two people are face to face in a room, one sitting in front of a window or door, the other sitting in front of a wall, the one with the wall behind will be in the more powerful position.

Excessively heavy beams overhead oppress chi and generate sha. It is not advisable to sleep or sit under an excessively heavy beam. If a beam looks or feels oppressive, you can hang a lantern, chandelier, or mobile from it to help transform its chi. You can also affix an ornament to it. One of my clients glued a red terra-cotta sun to such a beam in her apartment. It looked wonderful.

Structural columns anywhere but at the corners of a room block chi and generate sha. An exposed column standing in the room can be mirrored or camouflaged with standing plants, or, if the area is large enough, resolved by using a screen to divide the room. An exposed column can also be made into an object of art. One of my clients painted a spiraling blue dragon on the large cylindrical column in his living room.

Too many doors or windows in a room dissipate chi. Close off the least needed door or doors and treat the windows with blinds or curtains to help contain the chi.

If there is a pleasing or auspicious view outside a window, such as a body of water, a stand of trees, a garden, or beautiful vista, you can draw it in with a well-placed mirror so that you can see it from your favorite chair. You can also complement auspicious views by echoing their subject matter within. You can complement an outdoor garden with an indoor bonsai garden or a painting of a garden, and you can complement a river view with a painting of a water scene.

Fish tanks mean good fortune, and are traditionally used to ward off sha. If you use a fish tank to ward off sha, it should always have six red fish and one black fish, and should be placed across from the window through which secret arrows, as listed in chapter 2, are detected.

EXERCISE

You will need a fresh copy of your floor plan and a pencil for this exercise.

To ascertain how the chi circulates through your home, draw a smooth, continuous line, like an imaginary stream, through your floor plan, beginning at the main door and flowing through and around every room, as suggested by figure 111. Make sure your line follows the contours of each room and that it doesn't cut across the middle of your space or of any of the individual rooms. As you draw, let the line flow out and back in through all the windows. Spend some time experimenting with different ways of seeing this stream of chi. When your drawing is complete, you will have a basic overall plan for the arrangement of your furniture and decor.

(fig. 111)

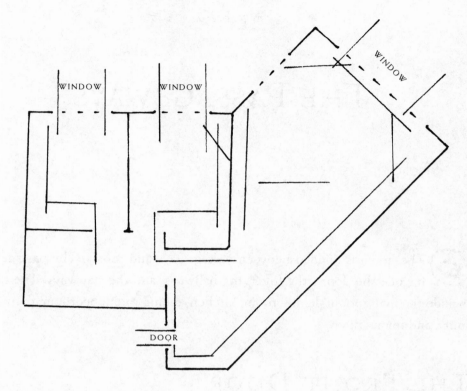

WINDOW

WINDOW

WINDOW

DOOR

THE PASSAGEWAYS

The home is divided between passageways and rooms. The passageways include the doors, the foyer, the hallways, and the stairways. The rooms include the living room, family room, kitchen, dining room, bedroom, bathroom, study, and home office.

THE FRONT DOOR

The first and most important of the passageways to consider is the front or main door. In addition to all that was discussed previously about its compass direction and relation to your birth star, you need to look at the main door, first in relation to what is outside, especially if the door opens to the street or to open country-side. Then you need to look at the main door in relation to what is inside. What you see upon first entering will have a subtle effect upon your mental state and therefore upon your health and fortunes.

If your home has more than one entrance, and you enter and exit almost always through a door other than the official front door, you should consider the door you habitually use to be your main door. The way you enter and exit determines your experience of your home.

The Door in Relation to the Outside

An obstacle of any kind in front of the door, whether it be a land formation, a hedge, a tree, a lamppost, a pole, etc., is undesirable.

A large obstacle positioned directly in front of the doorway blocks the entry of chi, and therefore of wealth. If there is an immovable object such as a lamppost directly in front of your doorway, you can balance it by placing other objects, such as potted trees or statues on either side of the door, as shown in figure 112, or placing a complementary object, such as a tree, on the other side of the house, as shown in figure 113.

(fig. 112)   *(fig. 113)*

LAMPPOST

LAMPPOST

Trees or bushes growing too close to the doorway and windows hamper movement and strangle the chi of the house and should be removed.

It is desirable to have the door facing flat land or land that slopes gently down. For this reason, I have told clients to switch the main doorway from one side of the house to another. There should not be a rising slope in front of the door. Climbing up a hill to get out of the house tells of obstacles and delays in your worldly affairs.

A path or driveway that leads directly to a door at ground level sends secret arrows into the house, as shown in figure 114.

To remedy this problem, change the shape of the path or driveway to slow down the approach to the house, as shown in figure 115, or hang a ba gua mirror,

151

face out, over the door. You can also mirror the wall directly facing the doorway in the foyer to repel the secret arrows.

(fig. 114) *(fig. 115)*

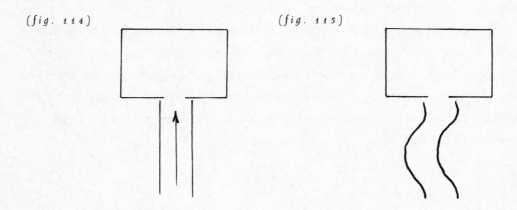

A path leading directly to a door, which is approached by steps, will not send secret arrows into the house because the steps take the doorway out of the line of sha. Nevertheless, the path should be comfortably wide.

Secret arrows that come against a house situated at the end of a blind alley, a cul-de-sac, or at the crosspoint of a T-junction can be controlled by planting a hedge of bushes or trees between the house and the roadway, or, if there isn't enough space, by placing a mirror on the wall of the foyer directly facing the door-way. Hanging a wind chime in the entrance will also help, but to a lesser degree.

THE DOOR IN RELATION TO THE INSIDE

Looking at the door in relation to the inside, check that it does not open to a wall, as shown in figure 116. This produces the effect of confinement. Conversely, when the door opens away from the wall, as shown in figure 117, it produces the effect of ease.

(fig. 116) *(fig. 117)*

If, upon opening the front door, you see out the back door or back windows, the chi, instead of flowing calmly throughout the entire space of your home, shoots out like an arrow through the back door or window. This produces the effect of splitting your home apart and draining it of chi. To remedy this, place a screen, curtain, shelving unit, or other construction between the front and back doors to divert the stream of chi into the house; and in the case of a window, hang venetian blinds or curtains. Even lace or sheer curtains are fine.

A wall partition seen from the main door, as shown in figure 118, produces the effect of imbalance. To resolve the unbalanced effect, put a full-length mirror or beautiful ornament that attracts attention on the obstructing side, as shown in figure 119. Better yet, use a screen or other construction, providing there is enough room, as shown in figure 120.

(fig. 1 1 8)   *(fig. 1 1 9)*   *(fig. 1 2 0)*

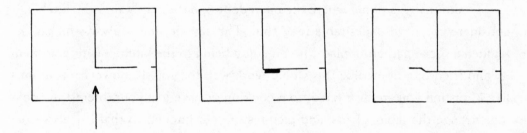

UPON ENTERING YOUR HOME

It is important to take note of what you see when you first open the door. The ideal would be a beautifully decorated foyer or entrance hall with common rooms (yang) close by, and private rooms (yin) farther back. If you are among the many who do not have this ideal layout, there are ways to mitigate your problems.

If, upon opening the main door, you can see into a bedroom, as shown in figure 121, the bedroom is too exposed to outside disturbances. To remedy this, put a full-length mirror on the outside of the bedroom door to ward off negative chi from the outside, and/or, hang a curtain to conceal the door at least partially from view if the space permits.

153

(*fig. 121*)

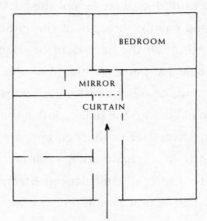

Looking into an open kitchen upon first entering your home is also less than desirable because it draws your attention unduly to food. Cover the entrance to the kitchen with either swinging doors, a beaded curtain, or a Japanese-style curtain-door.

Traditionally, a home where the main door opens directly into the kitchen is considered to have undesirable feng shui. This layout almost always makes the kitchen a social gathering place. If you enjoy being in the kitchen with your family and friends, a home like this would work well for you. If, however, you don't like it, or find you are distracted from cooking or have lost your interest in cooking, arrange the table, chairs, and pictures in your kitchen so that it feels secure and comfortable. It will also help matters if you hang wind chimes near the doorway, or hang a string of bells from the hinges of the door to dispel negative chi.

It is undesirable to have the main door too close to the dining area, as shown in figure 122; it interferes with nourishment. In a space such as this, try to move the dining area away from the main door to where the chi is calmer, or put up a screen if there is enough room for one.

(*fig. 122*)

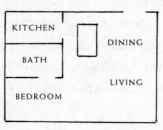

Although it is perfectly fine to see the living room from the main door, when the door opens directly into the living room, it exposes the room too much to the outside and makes much of the area around the door useless. Objects such as wall units, bookcases, or, if there is sufficient light, large standing plants can be placed near the door to create a feeling of privacy and containment, as well as make the area more functional.

Many people enter their private houses from the garage into a stairwell or utility room. This is a most stressful way to enter the house because it brings in noxious fumes and dirt. Habitually entering and leaving your house via an interior stairwell from which there are steps going up and down creates a sense of confusion about direction and could result in accidents. It also causes the occupants of the house to feel cramped and unsettled.

The entrance to many city brownstones is situated at the top of a flight of stairs that rise up from the sidewalk. This is very good feng shui. When the entrance to the house is above the street, it gives the occupants the feeling of being at a secure distance from the activity of the street.

If the entrance to your home is below street level and you have to walk down a few steps from the sidewalk to enter your home, the chi of your home is somewhat depressed. You can easily remedy this condition by planting shrubs—especially evergreens—and flowers around the entrance.

THE FOYER

The foyer is the reception area and place of transition between what is outside and what is inside. Ideally, a foyer should open on a front room or living room. A home with a real foyer naturally feels more private and peaceful than one without a foyer.

If the foyer is small or narrow, it should be painted a light color and be softly lit. You can also use a mirror to good effect. The placement of the mirror is very important. It should not face the door, unless there is a problem of sha coming from outside, because visitors will be confronted with their reflection, which may cause them to feel unwelcome. It is better to place the mirror to the side of the door to reflect what is inside the house or apartment.

If the foyer is too small to use a mirror, hang a picture or textile with minute and interesting details facing the doorway, so that visitors will want to come close and look at it.

Be careful about putting furniture in a small foyer. Avoid cluttering and oppressing the entryway.

If the foyer is spacious enough, a table with an ornamental mirror hanging above it may be positioned to face the door with no ill effect.

HALLWAYS

Hallways are like arteries that convey nourishment to the different organs of the body. The hallways are channels through which chi moves from room to room. When the hallways are open and clear, the entire dwelling breathes freely and is filled with healthy chi. But when hallways are blocked or cluttered, the functioning of the different rooms becomes weakened and the house becomes an unhealthy place in which to live.

A hallway that is long and narrow, as shown in figure 123, generates secret arrows. To remedy this, place a series of mirrors along one of the walls to slow down the movement of the chi, change its course from being straight to undulant, and create a more spacious feeling, as shown in figure 124. You could also hang a few pictures on the wall opposite the mirrors to create an interesting effect.

(fig. 123) *(fig. 124)*

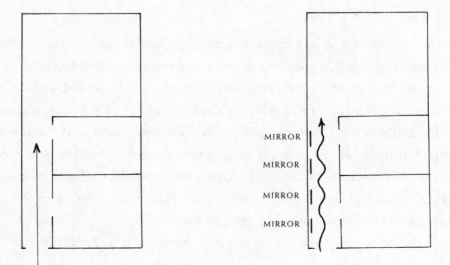

A hallway that has too many doors is potentially chaotic. If you are designing a house, it is best to place the doors in a hallway at regularly alternating intervals, as shown in figure 125. This type of arrangement allows for smooth and easy movement.

Doors directly facing one another, as shown in figure 126, suggest lack of privacy and conflict. Subdued colors and soft lighting, however, can be effectively used to neutralize this condition.

(fig. 125)   *(fig. 126)*

Doors that partially overlap, as shown in figure 127, suggest discord and strife. To remedy this, place mirrors extending from the top of the door to the baseboard along the sides, as shown in figure 128, to fill out the overlapping areas. Subdued colors and soft lighting should be used as well.

(fig. 127)   *(fig. 128)*

A hallway where the doors are crowded on one end, as shown in figure 129, is extremely discordant and suggests hostility between the people using the different rooms. Its remedy is identical to that of figure 126.

157

(fig. 129)

DOOR

DOOR

DOOR

In a hallway where doors open out and bang into each other, there is the danger of injury. The remedy really depends on the situation. The doors can be taken off and replaced with sliding or folding doors, or a curtain or louvered door can be used. However, the ideal way to remedy hallways in which the doors are in such conflict is to make structural alterations to relocate the different doors.

A room situated at the end of a long hallway receives secret arrows much in the same way as a house does at the end of a blind alley. To remedy this problem, put a full-length mirror on the side of the door that faces the hallway.

If a hallway is divided into segments by large structural beams running across the width of its ceiling, place decorative ornaments on the beams to make them into an attractive feature.

INTERIOR STAIRWAYS

Interior stairways can create a number of problems according to their location and structural design.

A stairway that runs directly toward the front, side, or back door, as shown in figure 130, causes chi to run out the door, indicating the loss of money.

There are two ways to remedy this problem. The first and best way is to redesign the stairs to turn away from the door, as shown in figure 131. The second way is to draw the attention upward by hanging a brightly colored picture or ornament on the wall of the upper landing that can be seen from below and by putting a mirror on the door wall to reflect the stairs.

(fig. 130)   (fig. 131)

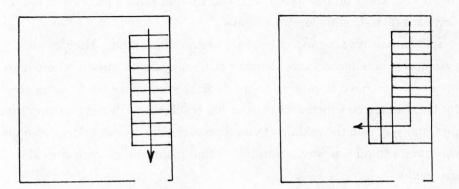

If, upon entering the house, you face stairs going up on one side and down on the other, as shown in figure 132, you are confronted by a vortex that can lead to a sense of confused direction in life.

Provided that the foyer is deep enough, this problem can be remedied by installing sliding shoji screens or doors made with frosted glass in front of the stairways, so that they can be opened from either side.

If the foyer is too shallow, as in figure 133, the problem can be remedied by constructing a vestibule or by hanging curtains over at least the opening to the stairs going down.

(fig. 132)   (fig. 133)

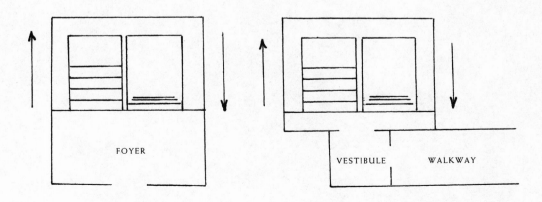

Stairs should have risers. If there are no risers there may be a danger of accidents. If your stairs do not have risers, you can put potted plants and flood lights underneath them to shine up from below.

Spiral stairways save space, but they are also hazardous. They create a gyrating effect that could lead to accidents or distressing conditions in different areas of your life. If you have a spiral stairway, look at your space while using the eight point method to see which area of your life is subject to distressing conditions. If a spiral stairway is in the middle of your home, it will adversely affect your vitality. If you have a spiral stairway, try to put potted plants underneath it to absorb the negative chi.

EXERCISES

1. Take note of what you see upon first opening your door and looking into your house or apartment. What impression does it make? Does it please you? If not, can you define the problem? What can you do to correct it? If necessary, review the problems and treatments discussed above.

2. Make sure that all the passageways in your home, the doorways, the foyer, the hallways and stairways, are unobstructed and free of hazardous conditions.

THE BEDROOM AND BATH

◯ THE BEDROOM

The bedroom is the most intimate place in your home. It should be relaxing and calming, and although it should be neither too small nor too large, its size is not as important as the quality of its chi. If the chi of your bedroom is either depressed or too active, it will have adverse effects on both your inner and outer life. If the room seems too small, you can compensate for its size by decorating it with pale and subdued hues. If, on the other hand, it seems too large, you can decorate it with vivid and rich hues to give it a feeling of closeness.

In addition to the bed, the bedroom furniture may include one or two night-stands, a bureau, a few chairs, a chest, a chaise longue or love seat, and perhaps a small writing table.

THE PLACEMENT OF THE BED

The placement of the bed is the most important decision to make in the home. Your bed is where you sleep and recuperate your energy every night. Where you place your bed very much determines how well you rest. Many times after changing the position of my clients' beds, they reported to me how much their sleep had improved.

Let's consider the different areas of the bedroom in relation to the door and windows to decide upon the best placement for the bed.

There are a number of bed positions to avoid. The worst position is when its foot points directly out the door, as shown in figure 134. This symbolizes death, because corpses are traditionally removed from a room feet first.

Avoid placing the bed so that the path of chi coming in from the doorway cuts across it to disturb your sleep, as shown in figure 135.

(fig. 1 3 4)   *(fig. 1 3 5)*

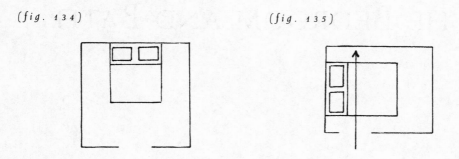

Do not place the head of the bed against or directly under a window, as shown in figure 136. Not only is this an insecure position, but you are exposed to drafts.

Try to avoid placing the bed so that its foot points directly out a window, as shown in figure 137.

(fig. 1 3 6)   *(fig. 1 3 7)*

The bed should not be placed under a severely sloping ceiling, as shown in figure 138; the chi of whomever sleeps there will be depressed.

(fig. 1 3 8)

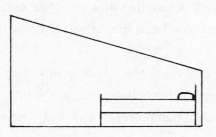

Avoid placing the bed so that you can only get in and out of it on one side, as shown in figures 139 and 140, unless you wish to be alone. There really should be enough room to get in and out of both sides of the bed for it to be shared comfortably. The closest distance between the side of the bed and the wall should be no less than two feet.

(fig. 1 3 9)

(fig. 1 4 0)

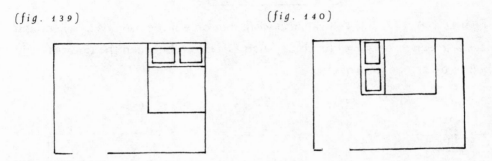

In addition, avoid placing the bed under a skylight, a heavy construction beam, or anything hanging overhead.

Figures 141 through 145 show the best placements for the bed. Note that none of them are in conflict with the doorway.

(fig. 1 4 1)

(fig. 1 4 2)

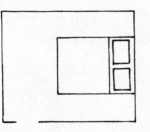

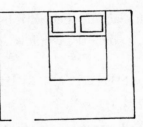

(fig. 1 4 3)

(fig. 1 4 4)

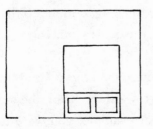

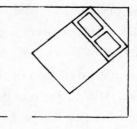

(fig. 145)

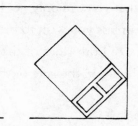

Figures 146, 147, and 148 can also work, but only if the room is large enough to place a screen or article of furniture, such as a chest, between the doorway and the bed to divert the flow of chi.

(fig. 146)   *(fig. 147)*   *(fig. 148)*

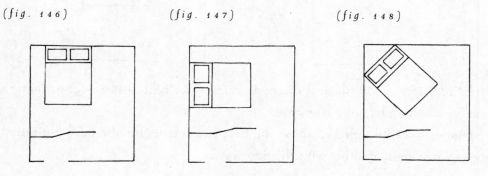

If you place the bed with its foot to the window as shown in figure 137, you will need to cover the window with either a venetian blind or curtains.

ALIGNING YOUR BED TO YOUR BIRTH STAR AND LUCKY STARS

You may find that there is more than one area in your bedroom that is good for the placement of your bed. Consult your personal data list. If one of these areas allows you to align your bed to a compass direction that harmonizes with your birth or lucky star, you should use it. If you are a couple, try to align your bed to the direction of a lucky star that you share in common, or to the compass direction of a star that harmonizes with both of your birth stars.

The compass direction of the bed is always determined by its head. In other words, if you stand at the foot of the bed and look toward the head, the direction you are facing is that of the bed's alignment. If, for example, you were to align your bed to the east, you would position it so that when standing at its foot and looking toward its head, you would be facing east.

PLACING YOUR BED IN AN AREA OF POSITIVE CHI

In addition to the possibilities of placement and alignment discussed above, you can also consider the possibility of placing the bed in an area of positive chi as defined by the compass direction of the bedroom doorway.

To locate the positive areas correctly, first read the direction of the bedroom door with your compass, remembering to look out, not in. Then locate the middle of the room, and delineate the eight areas radiating out from it.

If the door faces **north,** the areas to the east, southeast, and south of the middle of the room are the most positive.

If the door faces **northeast,** the areas to the southwest, west, and northwest of the middle of the room are the most positive.

If the door faces **east,** the areas to the southeast, south, and north of the middle of the room are the most positive.

If the door faces **southeast,** the areas to the south, north, and east of the middle of the room are the most positive.

If the door faces **south,** the areas to the north, east, and southeast of the middle of the room are the most positive.

If the door faces **southwest,** the areas to the west, northwest, and northeast of the middle of the room are the most positive.

If the door faces **west,** the areas to the northwest, northeast, and southwest of the middle of the room are the most positive.

If the door faces **northwest,** the areas to the northeast, southwest, and west of the middle of the room are the most positive.

If you cannot use one of the areas of positive chi as defined by the compass direction of your bedroom doorway, please refer to the method of harmonizing the chi of your space with the colors discussed in chapter 14. By harmonizing the chi of the room with colors, you effectively bring the eight areas of the room into a positive relationship with the chi of the doorway.

To demonstrate the placement and alignment of the bed let's look at the following examples:

TOM

Tom's birth star is 3 Wood, his lucky star is 1 Water, and his bedroom door faces west. His birth and lucky stars show us that his most favorable alignments are to the north, east, southeast, and south.

The most positive areas in Tom's bedroom are the northwest, northeast, and southwest areas, as delineated in figure 149. The northeast area appears to be the best in relation to the doorway. The bed placed in the northeast area with its head pointing north, the compass direction of Tom's lucky star, is the best placement for his bed.

(fig. 149)

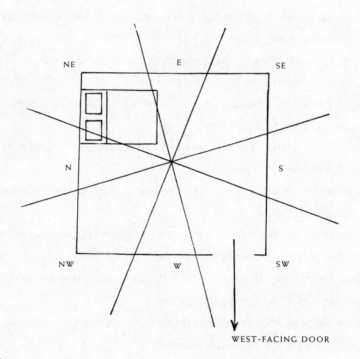

WEST-FACING DOOR

FRED

Fred's birth star is 4 Wood, his lucky star is 9 Fire, and his bedroom door faces southeast. His birth and lucky stars show us that his most favorable alignments are to the north, east, southeast, and south.

As determined by the compass direction of the door, shown in figure 150, the areas of positive chi in the room are in the north, east, southeast, and south. However, none of these areas can be used suitably for the placement of Fred's bed. The most suitable placement for the bed, relative to the doorway, is in the northeast area. The element of the northeast, Earth, however, is out of harmony with the element of the southeast-facing door, Wood. Therefore, the bed, placed in the northeast area, should have a purple or red bedspread to bring it into complete harmony with the chi of the doorway.

(fig. 150)

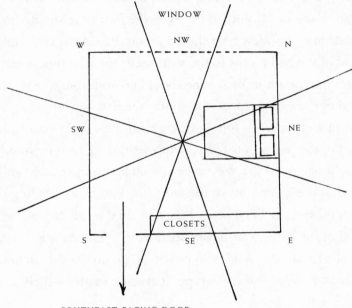

SOUTHEAST-FACING DOOR

For a Couple Sharing a Bed

If you are part of a couple, it is important for you to determine who goes on which side of the bed. If you are positioned side by side correctly, a current of positive chi will flow between you, much like that which occurs when two magnets are joined, while incorrect positioning will generate a repelling force between you that may contribute to conflicts in your relationship.

According to your birth star, you are one of two types, the East type or the West type. If your birth star is 1 Water, 3 Wood, 4 Wood, or 9 Fire, you are an East type. If your birth star is 2 Earth, 5 Earth, 6 Metal, 7 Metal, or 8 Earth, you are a West type.

167

How to Determine Who Goes on Which Side of the Bed

Stand at the foot of the bed with your compass and look toward the head. If the head of the bed is to the **north**, the East type should go on the side to your right hand and the West type should go on the side to your left hand.

If the head of the bed points to the **northeast**, the East type should go on the side to your left hand and the West type should go on the side to your right hand.

If the head of the bed points to the **east**, the East type should go on the side to your left hand and the West type should go on the side to your right hand.

If the head of the bed points to the **southeast**, the East type should go on the side to your left hand and the West type should go on the side to your right hand.

If the head of the bed points to the **south**, the East type should go on the side to your left hand and the West type should go on the side to your right hand.

If the head of the bed points to the **southwest**, the East type should go on the side to your right hand and the West type should go on the side to your left hand.

If the head of the bed points to the **west**, the East type should go on the side to your right hand and the West type should go on the side to your left hand.

If the head of the bed points to the **northwest**, the East type should go on the side to your right hand and the West type should go on the side to your left hand.

If the two of you are the same type, it doesn't matter which side you take; either way the energy is good.

Bedroom Furnishings

The placement of the other pieces of furniture should be in harmony with the bed.

Make sure you do not see sharp corners pointing at you when lying in bed.

Absolutely avoid cluttering the room.

Keep the lines balanced, simple, and graceful.

Avoid hanging a mirror opposite the window—it will activate the chi of the room too much. Avoid placing mirrors where you can see yourself when lying in bed; mirrors will disturb your rest. It is generally advisable to keep as few mirrors as possible in the bedroom. Mirrors activate chi. The bedroom should be as calm as possible.

It is best not to have a television set or other electronic device in the bedroom. Sleeping with the television on or spending a lot of time watching it before going to sleep causes mental depression. If you must have a television in the bedroom, it is better to keep it in a cabinet with doors you can shut before going to sleep.

If you have a closet or wardrobe at the marriage point in your bedroom, make sure it is filled with attractive clothes. You can also decorate it, or the wall space next to it, with pictures suggestive of love.

If you have a closet or wardrobe at the money point in your bedroom, fill it with fine clothes as well, and decorate it, or the wall space next to it, with pictures suggestive of abundance.

A standing plant next to a wardrobe at either of these points will also help generate positive chi and help integrate the wardrobe into the room.

Try to arrange an intimate sitting area and/or keep a beautiful vase with fresh flowers on a small table or stand at the marriage point.

If you are moving into a new place, throw out your mattress and buy a new one; it will change your luck for the better.

THE BATHROOM

The treatment of the bathroom is a fairly simple matter. There are two things to consider, namely where it is and its condition.

It is considered bad feng shui to have a bathroom in the northeast, the west, and the middle areas of your home.

A bathroom in the northeast area is bad because it attracts spirits of disease and decay. If you have a bathroom in the northeast, paint it entirely white, use white furnishings, and place a full-length mirror on the outside of the bathroom door to repel negative chi.

A bathroom in the west area is unfortunate for women. If you have a bathroom in the west, paint it gold, ocher, or yellow, floor it with stone or clay tile, and decorate it with clay pots and jars to give an earthy feeling. You should also place a full-length mirror on the outside of its door.

A bathroom in the middle of a house depresses the chi of the entire house. If you have a bathroom in the middle of your home, place a full-length mirror on the outside of the door to repel negative chi and place mirrors inside the bathroom on the walls so that they reflect one another and activate positive chi. Ideally, you should be able to put mirrors on all four walls. Mirrors on two opposing walls, however, are sufficient to activate the chi.

Make sure the plumbing in the bathroom is in good repair. Leaking faucets and pipes presage losses of money.

If the bathroom has no windows, you should treat it in exactly the same way as you would a bathroom in the middle of the house; the activation of positive chi will compensate for the lack of circulating air.

If a bathroom is at the money point of your home, put a full-length mirror on the outside of the bathroom door to repel negative chi, and make sure that the plumbing is in perfect order. Leaking water means your money is running out. If a bathroom is at the marriage point of your home, make it a special place where you can cultivate your health and beauty.

EXERCISES

Use the following steps to arrange your bedroom furniture:

1. Consider the placement of your bed in different areas in the room relative to the door and windows.

2. If you find several areas in the room that are good for the placement of your bed, refer to your personal data list to see if one of these areas allows you to align your bed in a compass direction that is harmonious with your birth star or in the compass direction of one of your lucky stars.

3. See if it is possible to place your bed in an area of positive chi, as determined by the compass direction of the doorway of the room. If you cannot use one of the areas of positive chi, refer to the method of balancing the chi of your space with the colors discussed in chapter 14. Once you have the space harmoniously balanced, it is entirely filled with positive chi.

4. Once you have found the key place and alignment for your bed, arrange all the other articles of furniture in your bedroom to complement it.

The Common Rooms

The common rooms include the living room, the family room, the kitchen, and the dining room. Let's discuss each in turn.

The Living Room

The living room is the most yang and public room in the home. It should be warm and cheerful, welcoming and comfortable. It is meant to bring about opportunities for social interaction for you and your guests and should be decorated with your most aesthetically pleasing possessions. Its furnishings, in addition to couches, chairs, tables, and lamps, may include a stereo, a TV, a piano, various works of art, and plants.

The living room can be organized around the following: one or more of the eight points; the power point, which is always diagonally across from the doorway; a special feature such as a fireplace; or an interesting urban or garden view.

If you organize the living room around one or more of the eight points, your best choices are the money, marriage, and friends points, respectively. Try to use the money point as your focal point. If the room is large enough for you to arrange the furniture around two points, let the larger arrangement go around the money point.

To give you a general idea, place a beautiful work of art, a standing plant, or a television set in the area of the money point, and arrange the furniture around it, as suggested in figure 151.

You might also arrange the room around its power point, diagonally across from the doorway, as shown in figure 152. This will give you command over the room.

(fig. 151)   (fig. 152)

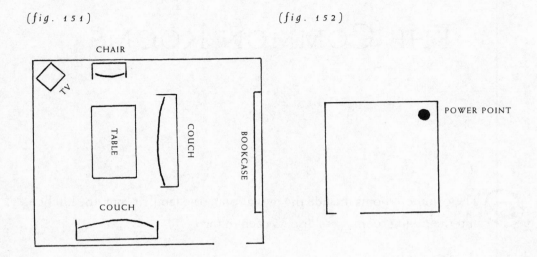

If you prefer to organize the room around a special view, such as a garden, locate the best siting point or points in the room and place your favorite chairs or couches at these points so that anyone who sits there may enjoy the view. Then arrange the rest of the furniture to complement the chairs and/or couches that you have placed at these special siting points.

THE ARRANGEMENT OF THE FURNITURE

Do not position the host's chair or main couch so that it looks directly out the door. If you are the host, you will feel too exposed, and anyone walking into the room will feel confronted by you.

It is best not to position the main chair or couch so that it faces directly out a window; this also will cause you to feel too exposed.

Do not position the main chair or couch so that its back is to the door or to a window. This will make you feel ill at ease or threatened.

Although chairs and couches for guests may be positioned with their backs to the windows or doorway, it is better to position them with their backs to the walls. Walls serve as protective barriers.

Chairs and couches should be positioned in harmonious alignments with the doors and windows to generate a feeling of easy movement in the room.

Couches directly facing one another, as shown in figure 153, bring people into intensive communication. It works well for people who are intimately involved, but might be too stressful for people who are not. If you have couches that directly face one another and can't place them any other way, you can ease their intensity with soft lighting. The seating configurations shown in figures 154 and 155 are more relaxed than that shown in figure 153.

(fig. 153)   *(fig. 154)*   *(fig. 155)*

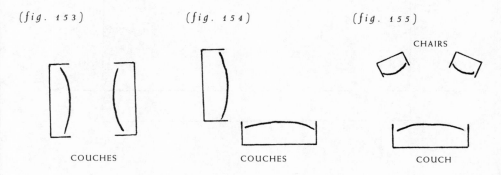

COUCHES   COUCHES   COUCH

Figure 155 is called a bow shape. It works well anywhere except in front of the doorway of an adjoining room, where it will send secret arrows into the adjoining room.

Try to position your favorite chair so that its back is to the compass direction of one of your lucky stars. Sitting with your lucky star to your back brings its invigorating energy into your body.

There are three situations when the chi runs through and splits up the room that must be remedied. When one window directly opposes another window, use blinds or curtains on one or both. When a door directly opposes a window, use blinds or curtains on the window. When a door directly opposes another door, use a screen to conceal one of the doors if the screen doesn't obstruct movement.

Figure 156 shows another way to resolve the problem of doors facing doors. The figure shows a living room, which also doubles as a passageway to other rooms. As you can see, the living area is much smaller than the actual size of the room.

As the passageways have to remain open, the room was arranged to create a sense of intimacy in a clearly defined area while allowing free movement through the rest of the room, as shown in figure 157. The shape of the arrangement of the furniture together with the fireplace describes an octagon. A most auspicious form, the octagon symbolizes the union of heaven and earth.

(fig. 156)

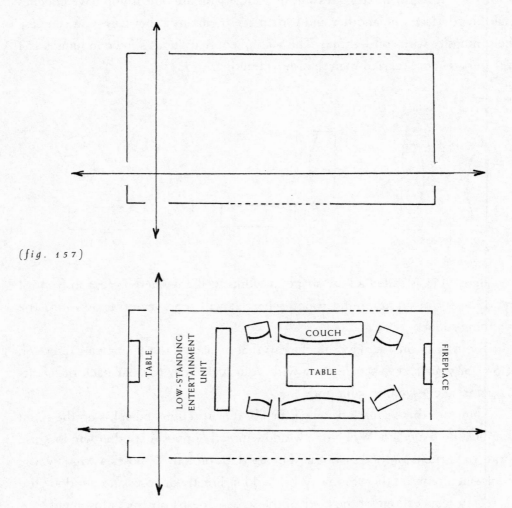

(fig. 157)

Contrary to the characteristic nature of a living room, a sunken living room is yin. Nonetheless, as sunkenness implies the element Water, and as Water generates Wood, it can be transformed to yang by placing potted plants, especially tall standing plants, about the room. If the room has insufficient light, artificial lighting should be installed. Another alternative is to use trees with leaves made of silk.

THE FAMILY ROOM

The family room should be arranged in a completely informal way so that everyone will be able to relax and enjoy being there together. The furniture should be useful, comfortable, and movable to allow for different activities such as games, watching television, and so forth. Because it is a very active area filled with cheerfulness and warmth, the family room should have light colors and be filled with decorations and mementos.

If you want to organize anything like a game table or entertainment unit around any of the eight points, you might consider using the family and children points. You could also put pictures of family members and family gatherings at the family point.

You could use the family room as a barometer for gaining insight into the well-being of the various family members according to the following method:

Find the middle of the room and then the eight areas using your compass. Each area represents a family member. The southwest area represents mother; the northwest area represents father; the east represents the eldest son; the north the middle son; the northeast area the youngest son; the southeast represents the eldest daughter; the south the middle daughter; and the west area the youngest daughter. If you have one son and/or one daughter, the east represents your son and the southeast represents your daughter. If you have two sons and/or two daughters, the east represents the elder son, the northeast represents the younger son, the southeast represents the elder daughter, and the west represents the younger daughter.

The room is likely to be in a continuous state of flux, and you need to be aware of repetitious accumulation of clutter in any one area. This will point to complicated developments in the life of whomever that area represents.

THE KITCHEN

The cauldron, or cooking vessel, called the *ting* in Chinese, is the very symbol of civilization. In ancient times the ting was used in religious festivals to feed everyone, including the living, the ancestors, and the host of heaven.

The kitchen is the place where food is prepared, and because food supports life, the kitchen symbolizes love, nurture, knowledge, wealth—all that fosters life.

One of the main reasons for the disintegration of closely knit relationships and of family life in our society is that our nourishment is habitually disrupted or ignored. Cooking is an expression of support. Attention to food preparation, and therefore to the provision of nourishment, is at the very core of family life, and when done with love and devotion, brings good fortune to all the family members.

The elements in the kitchen are Fire and Water: Fire for the stove, Water for the sink and refrigerator. As Fire and Water suggest potential conflict, you need to be aware of the relative placements of the stove, sink, and refrigerator.

In a nutshell, sha is generated when the sink and refrigerator are adjacent to, or in opposition to, the stove.

If the stove or wall oven is positioned between the sink and refrigerator, as in figure 158; if it is opposite the sink and refrigerator, as in figure 159; or if it is in an island in the middle of the room, as in figure 160, Fire is oppressed by Water, which indicates lack of contentment, obstacles to financial growth, and domestic quarrels.

If the stove, sink, and refrigerator are placed in a line, as in figure 161, Fire is overwhelmed by Water and suggests losing one's way in life through confusion and the inability to see things as they actually are.

(fig. 158)   (fig. 159)

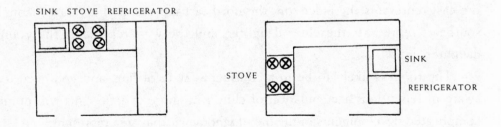

To remedy these conditions, introduce the element that comes between Fire and Water—Wood, which, as you may recall, is symbolized by the colors green and light blue.

In an arrangement similar to those described in figures 158 and 161, place an ornamental dish or configuration of tiles of green or light blue on the wall between the stove and the sink, or the stove and the refrigerator. In an arrangement similar to those described in figures 159 and 160, place a green or blue floor mat between the stove and the other appliances, or else cover the entire floor with green or blue tiles.

(fig. 160)   *(fig. 161)*

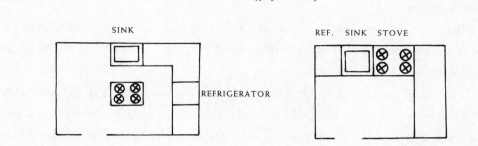

The kitchen should not be a completely open area or passageway through which people can come and go freely and distract you when you are cooking. To distract the cook means to interfere with the provision of nourishment. Lack of proper nourishment points to lack of love, learning, and money. If your kitchen is in an open area, you can create a boundary in front of it with a table or construct a counter, which could also serve as an eating area.

A door directly behind or to the side of the stove, as shown in figure 162, can cause you to feel uneasy while cooking.

(fig. 162)

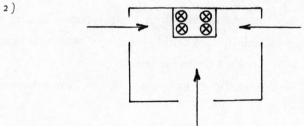

The door behind the stove is worse than the door to the side. To remedy its adverse effect, place a mirror on the wall so that when standing at the stove you will be able to see what is behind you, and therefore have command over the door.

The stove should neither be placed where the ventilation and lighting are poor, nor under a window or skylight where it might become drafty.

177

THE DINING ROOM

The dining room, like the kitchen, ideally should be an enclosed room. It should not be open to distractions, but should be a quiet and pleasant, warm and cheerful place where you can come together with loved ones to share nourishing food and conversation.

The dining room should be comfortable and intimate, and should have no more than two doors, one from the kitchen and one from either the living room or the hallway.

The dining room should be decorated with cheerful works of art and with fresh flowers, its colors should be light, and it should not have too many windows, as they will generate too much activity. Nothing about the dining room should be distracting, irritating, or discomforting. If there are too many windows, cover at least some of them, in a symmetrical fashion, with either venetian blinds or curtains. Lace curtains can create a pleasant effect.

The furniture should consist of no more than the dining table, the chairs, and a sideboard. Put the table in the center of the room.

The chairs ideally should be placed with their backs to the walls, not to the windows or doors. They also should be even in number. Even numbers suggest pairs, and pairs suggest love, which is at the source of nourishment and nurturing. There is a Chinese proverb that says, "Happiness comes in pairs." Another says, "Pleasure shared is pleasure doubled."

In most modern houses and apartments there is no separate dining room. If, instead of a dining room, you only have a dining alcove or area, you need to create the same feeling in it as if it were a dining room.

If you have a dining alcove, as shown in figure 163, you can improve on it by defining it with standing plants.

If your dining area resembles figure 164, you can delineate it with the back of a couch or other piece of furniture. It will also help matters if the color of the dining area is set off from that of the living room area.

(*fig. 163*)   (*fig. 164*)

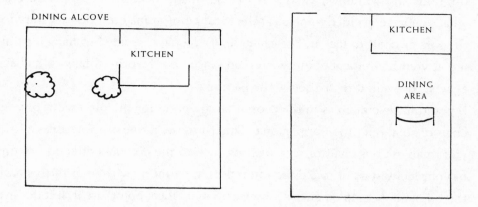

Table shapes have symbolic meanings. A round table symbolizes heaven's blessings; a square table means the blessings of earth; and the octagonal table symbolizes the gathering of heaven and earth with all their children. The circle, the square, and the octagon, as they have no place for the head of the table, show humbleness, compassion, and love. The rectangle and the oval, on the other hand, are hierarchical, formal, and less friendly. The octagonal table limits its seating to eight, which means you have to use it as a buffet table if you have more than eight people coming to dinner. A big round table, however, implies no number; it is the best for big, happy gatherings.

EXERCISES

Use the following steps to arrange the furniture of your living room:

1. Select the main focal point of the room. If the room has a fireplace, it should be the main focal point. If there is no fireplace, the main focal point could be one of the eight points, such as the money point or the marriage point.

2. If you don't have a fireplace, consider what to put at the main focal point. It might be a sofa, an entertainment unit, a piano, a piece of sculpture, a painting, a wall hanging, or a standing plant.

3. Select your main piece of furniture. It should either be your favorite sofa or your favorite chair.

4. Consider placing your chair or sofa in different areas in the room relative to the door and windows, as well as to your main focal point. Depending on what you have decided to place at the focal point, it may not be necessary for the sofa or chair to face it. For example, if you have decided to hang a painting at your main focal point, you could place your favorite sofa with its back against the wall, directly below the painting.

5. If you find several areas in the room that are good for the placement of your chair or sofa, refer to your personal data list to see if one of these areas allows you to align your chair or sofa with its back to the compass direction of one of your lucky stars or to a direction that is in harmony with your birth star. If this alignment complements your selected main focal point, use it. If it doesn't, consider changing the focal point.

6. Once you have found the key placement of your favorite chair or sofa and the main focal point of the room, arrange the other pieces of furniture around the focal point and in a balanced composition with your favorite chair or sofa.

THE STUDY AND
HOME OFFICE

◎ THE STUDY

The study is a room for reading, writing, and meditating. The chi of the study should be balanced between yin and yang; it should be both restful and conducive to work. The room should be neither too spacious nor too cramped, and its shape should be simple and easy on the eye.

The rectangular shape is best for the study. If your study is L-shaped, use one of the areas for your desk and the other for a sitting area. If your study has an irregular shape, use the methods discussed in chapters 12 and 13 to treat it.

Ideally, the view from the windows of the study should be pleasant. Your attention nonetheless should be drawn into the room for the sake of your creative work. If the view out of the windows is disturbing, if the windows face your neighbor's windows, or if they face a building that is dilapidated, a dead tree, railroad tracks, electrical wires, sharply pointed objects, or other causes of sha, hang curtains on the windows. Plants hung in the window or placed on the windowsill may also be used to good effect.

The atmosphere you want to generate in the study is calm and clear.

The furnishings that go into a study include a desk, or writing or drawing table, bookcases, file cabinets, shelves, a comfortable chair and/or couch, and works of art. The room should also have a rug. The rug should be deep blue, black, or other dark color. It should be of medium size in relation to the room and be placed at the center of the room, in line with the walls. A deep blue rug in the middle of the study is like a deep pool of water upon which to rest the eyes and reflect. The middle of the room should always be open. The open center symbolizes the unfathomable Tao.

The most significant piece of furniture in the study is the desk. You should determine the placement of the desk much in the same way you determined the placement of the bed as discussed in chapter 18.

The worst positions for the desk in relation to the doorway and windows are shown in figures 165 through 172.

(fig. 165)

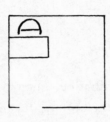

(fig. 166)

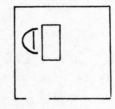

(fig. 167)

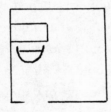

(fig. 168)

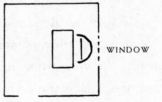

WINDOW

(fig. 169)

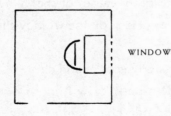

WINDOW

(fig. 170)

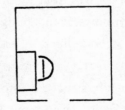

(fig. 171)   (fig. 172)

(fig. 171)   (fig. 172)

Do not place the desk directly in line with the door, either facing it (fig. 165), with it to your side (fig. 166), or with the chair positioned so that the door is behind you (fig. 167). Do not place the desk so that you sit with your back exposed to a window (fig. 168). Do not place the desk flat up against a window so that you face directly out of it (fig. 169). Do not place the desk where you feel cramped and bothered (fig. 170), confined and with a limited field of vision (fig. 171), or where there is a passageway behind you (fig. 172). Do not place the desk against a mirror.

The most commanding positions in the room are diagonally across from the doorway, as shown in figures 173, 174, and 175. The positions shown in figures 176, 177, and 178 also work very well.

(fig. 173)   (fig. 174)   (fig. 175)

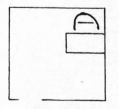

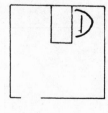

(fig. 176)   (fig. 177)   (fig. 178)

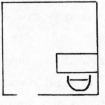

If the room is deep enough, the desk can be placed facing the doorway, or with its side to the doorway if you also place a screen or high-rising cabinetry between the doorway and the desk, as shown in figures 179 and 180.

(fig. 179)　　　　　　　　　　　　　　　*(fig. 180)*

CABINET　　　　　　　　　　　　　　SCREEN

For ease of the eye and the feeling of security, it is best to place the desk so that you sit with your back to a wall or corner. It is preferable to have the desk facing into the room rather than facing a wall.

If you decide to place the desk flat up against a wall, it is better, if you are right-handed, to have a window to your left, as in figure 181. If you are left-handed, it is better to have a window to your right, as in figure 182.

(fig. 181)　　　　　　　　　　　　　　*(fig. 182)*

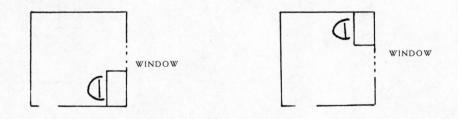

WINDOW　　　　　　　　　　　　　　WINDOW

The only case where it is good to have the desk against a window, provided no one can look in at you, is if when looking directly out you face due north, a most auspicious direction.

Try to place your desk so that when sitting at it, the compass direction of your lucky star, or a compass direction that is in harmony with your birth star, is to your back. For example, if your lucky star is 4 Wood, you would sit with your back to the southeast. If your birth star is 4 Wood, you could sit with your back either to the southeast, the north, the east, or the south.

Depending on your particular field of interest, you can also use the eight point method as a guide for the placement of the desk and related pieces of furniture.

The money, fame, friends, career, and knowledge points denote favorable areas for all commercial, financial, professional, and business interests.

The knowledge, marriage, fame, and friends points are favorable for scholarly, literary, and artistic interests.

The family, marriage, children, and friends points are favorable for all social interests.

The children point is favorable for anything relating specifically to children such as teaching, writing, and illustrating children's literature, designing toys, and inventing games, etc.

Once you determine the placement of the desk, you will need to consider the arrangement of the bookcases, filing cabinets, and works of art. The main rule is orderliness. The furniture should be conveniently and neatly placed to give the room a feeling of balance and ease. It should be easy to move about the room, and all information should be easily accessible. Avoid obstructing the windows, blocking the doors, and cluttering the corners. Arrange the bookcases and filing cabinets in straight lines and symmetrical configurations. Aim for simplicity. Think creatively. Trust your intuition.

The lighting in the study should be soft, with direct lighting, possibly provided by spot lighting, to read and write easily, especially at the desk and sitting area.

Avoid hanging plants above the desk or sitting area. Anything hanging directly overhead is to be avoided.

THE HOME OFFICE

The home office is akin to the study. However, where the chi of the study is always balanced between yin and yang, the home office may be balanced between yin and yang or be predominantly yang, depending on its use. Also, whereas the study should ideally be in a more or less secluded area of the house or apartment, the home office, if it is a place to receive clients and conduct business, should be close to the front door.

To arrange the home office correctly, work with the indications for the study and include the following:

If you practice one of the healing arts, the chi should be balanced between yin and yang. Try to place the couch, therapy table, or mat in one of the areas of positive chi, determined by the compass direction of the door of the room as discussed in chapter 18. If the room is not large enough to place a therapy table or mat in one of the areas of positive chi, place the therapy table or mat in the center of the room to provide ample space to work in.

If you are a therapist or counselor and your office is a room where you and your client sit facing each other at a table, place the table in the middle of the room if the room is not too large. Otherwise, choose a comfortable area away from the door where you can sit with your back to a wall, and where the client's chair is positioned to provide him or her with a sense of security.

If you are using the room as a business office where you receive customers, the chi should be yang. Place the customer's chair so that he sits with the door to his back. His chair should be slightly lower than yours so that he will look up to you.

If you use the room as a conference room, place the table in the middle of the room, or in a position where you can easily walk around it.

It is undesirable to place two desks face to face because they will generate too much tension between the people using them.

Lining up desks, one in front of the other, as shown in figure 183, as is done all too often in large corporations, will generate a line of sha from back to front. Figures 184, 185, and 186 show more pleasant arrangements.

(fig. 183)   (fig. 184)

(fig. 185)   (fig. 186)

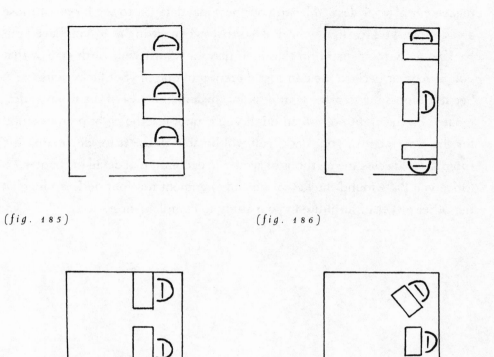

If you have people sitting side by side, assign them their places by the East type–West type method discussed in chapter 18. Stand at the front of the desk and face the chair to read the compass direction of the desk and chair correctly.

EXERCISES

Use the following steps to arrange the furniture in your study:

1. Consider placing your desk in different areas of the room relative to the door and windows.

2. If you find that there is more than one area in the room that is good for the placement of your desk, refer to your personal data list to see if one of those areas allows you to align your desk so that, when sitting at it, you have your back to a compass direction that is in harmony with your birth star or that you have your back to the compass direction of one of your lucky stars.

3. See if it is possible to place your desk in a meaningful area of the room as designated by the eight point method. If you cannot use the eight point method for the placement of your desk, you will be able to use it for decorating the room. I will discuss the methods of symbolic decoration in detail in chapter 22.

4. Once you have found the key place and alignment for your desk, arrange all the other pieces of furniture in your study to complement it.

c h a p t e r   2 1

STUDIO AND
ONE-BEDROOM APARTMENTS

⊙ THE STUDIO APARTMENT

A studio apartment can be much more difficult to arrange than a house or apartment with several rooms because you need to accommodate every aspect of your life in its single space. Size is a critical factor. The smaller the studio, the more likely it is to be cluttered or overfurnished.

The best shapes for a studio are the rectangle and the L-shape, providing the "L" isn't too small. Avoid placing a bed in an area that boxes it in on three, not to mention four, sides; the effect is stifling.

While the studio is essentially an open space, it contains yin and yang areas. The yin areas are those out of direct line with the door and windows. They are suitable for the placement of such articles of furniture as the bed and dining table. The yang areas, on the other hand, are more exposed, and are suitable for the living and working areas.

The first and most important piece of furniture to place is your bed. You should have no trouble finding the right place for it if you follow the guidelines in chapter 18. Use a shoji or other type of screen, a cabinet, or a chest of drawers to conceal the bed from the doorway. Be careful, however, not to cramp the bed. Once you have determined the place for the bed, you will need to consider how to arrange the room to accommodate your activities. If the studio displays a jumble of diverse interests and has no definite focus, it will contribute to confusion and anxiety. Try to aim for balanced and integrated organization.

If you want the studio to be a combination bedroom, living room, and work space, consider the placements of the bed and work table first. Follow the guidelines for the study in chapter 20 to arrange the work area. Make sure the work area feels open and comfortable. Once you have the bed and work table in place, arrange the couch and other living room furniture to complement them.

Sleeping alcoves in studios are often quite small. If you live in a studio with a sleeping alcove, be careful to arrange it to give the bed as much open space as possible. You should always be able to move about freely and comfortably.

THE ONE-BEDROOM APARTMENT

If you live in a one-bedroom apartment, keep your bedroom and living room separate. I have seen many one-bedroom apartments whose occupants had brought such things as computers and file cabinets into the bedroom. Small wonder they were overwhelmed by their work and had no room in their lives for their personal affairs.

If you have your work in your bedroom, you would do yourself a great favor by taking it out. Make the bedroom an entirely restful and intimate place. Use the living room instead of the bedroom for your work and living areas.

EXERCISES

Use the following steps to arrange your studio apartment:

1. Consider placing your bed in different areas in the room relative to the door and windows. The best place for the bed is where it feels most protected.

2. If you find there is more than one area in the room that is good for the placement of your bed, refer to your personal data list to see if one of these areas allows you to align your bed in a compass direction in harmony with your birth star or in the compass direction of one of your lucky stars.

3. Once you have decided on the placement of your bed, consider the placement of your next most important piece of furniture. If you work in your space, it would be your work table or desk. If not, it would be your sofa.

4. Once you have found the place for your desk or sofa, arrange all the other pieces of furniture to complement it and your bed.

FOCUSING YOUR GOALS: SYMBOLIC DECORATIONS

Once you have organized the colors and furniture placement of your home, you can go one step further and use symbolic decorations to focus your goals. The whole subject of symbolic decoration is vast and rich. It includes images, colors, plants, patterns, and groupings of objects.

The eight point method gives you eight symbolic directions that you can use effectively to focus your goals. First decide what area of your life and, therefore, which of the corresponding points you want to highlight. Then select the appropriate room. The living room is appropriate for all of the eight points, especially the money point. The bedroom is especially appropriate for the marriage point. The study is appropriate for the knowledge, money, fame, friends (including travel and communications), and career points.

If you want to develop your knowledge, put something inspirational at the knowledge point to represent your subject of interest. If you want to focus your attention on the family, hang pictures of family members at the family point. If your interest is prosperity, decorate the money point with symbols of wealth. If you are a performer or public figure and want to focus on your good reputation, hang something that inspires you to success at the reputation point. If your interests are romantic, hang the picture of your loved one or a picture that inspires romantic feelings at the marriage point. If you wish to focus on children, or wish to have children, hang pictures of children or pictures that remind you of childhood at the children point. If your interests are social, hang pictures of people and places that you love and admire at the friends point.

I once arranged a one-bedroom apartment for someone who was in the process of transforming her career from freelance writing to film production. We put her favorite film poster at the career point to inspire and encourage her as she went through the process of changing careers.

In another situation, I arranged the home office of someone who wanted to improve his financial status. We put a filing cabinet containing his financial records at the money point of his office, and put a Chinese stone sculpture of a toad with a coin in its mouth, a symbol of wealth, on top of the filing cabinet.

If you want to hang or place a special religious object or icon, use the direction of the door to find the most auspicious place for it. If the door to the room faces **south**, place the icon in the southeast area of the room. If the door faces **southwest**, place it in the west area of the room. If the door faces **west**, place it in the southwest area of the room. If the door faces **northwest**, place it in the northeast area of the room. If the door faces **north**, place it in the east area of the room. If the door faces **northeast**, place it in the northwest area of the room. If the door faces **east**, place it in the north area of the room. If the door faces **southeast**, place it in the south area of the room.

GENERAL SYMBOLS

The following is a list of traditional Chinese symbols with their meanings, which you can use to good effect.

SYMBOL	MEANING
Bats	Luck, happiness, and long life; they are often painted red, the color of joy
Bear	Strength and courage, protection against thieves
Bells	The breaking up of negative chi
Two birds	Romantic love
A broom	Sweeping away of trouble and vexation

Symbol	Meaning
Butterflies	Love and joy
Cicada	Rebirth, immortality, eternal youth, and joy
Coins	Prosperity
Conch shell	Prosperity
Cranes	Longevity and fidelity
Deer	Longevity and wealth
Dog	Protection and prosperity
Dove	Long life
Dragon	Fecundity, nobility, and creativity
Dragonfly	Impermanence and delicacy
Duck	Happiness
Elephant	Wisdom, strength, and power
Eagles and falcons	Farsightedness and daring
Goldfish	Success and abundance
Flowers	Wealth
Wild goose	Conjugal fidelity
Hare	Longevity and the vital essence of the moon
Horse	Perseverance and speed
Leopard	Bravery
Lion	Protection and defense
Monkey	Cleverness, health, and protection from evil
Old man	Long life
Peacock	Beauty
Pearls	Purity
Pheasant	Royalty, good fortune, and beauty
Phoenix	Beauty, love, peace, and prosperity
Quail	Courage
Swallows	Prosperity and success
Tiger	Sternness, courage, and ferocity
Toad	Wealth
Tortoise	Longevity
Unicorn	Longevity, fecundity, and joy

COLORS

The following is a list of colors with their symbolic meanings:

COLOR	MEANING
Yellow	The center and royalty
White	Purity
Blue/Black	The blessings of heaven
Green	Long life
Red	Joy, fame, and luck

PLANTS

The following is a list of trees and flowers with their symbolic meanings:

SYMBOL	MEANING
Apple	Peace and prosperity
Azalea	Feminine grace
Bamboo	Long life and youth
Cherry tree	Feminine beauty; for example, red lips
Chrysanthemum	Joyousness and long life
Cypress	Nobility
Jasmine	Sweetness, friendship, and love
Lotus	Fruitfulness
Magnolia	Feminine sweetness
Mulberry	Domestic peace
Narcissus	Good fortune and rejuvenation
Oak	Masculine strength and virility
Oleander	Beauty
Orange	Happiness and prosperity
Orchids	Love, beauty, fertility, strength, and gracefulness
Peach	Friendship, marriage, and immortality
Pear	Purity and long life

Symbol	Meaning
Peony	Love, wealth, and nobility
Persimmon	Joyousness
Pine	Long life
Plum blossom	Long life, youth, beauty, and an unconquerable spirit
Pomegranate	Many prosperous offspring
Rose	Beauty and love
Tangerine	Prosperity
Willow	Gentleness and feminine grace

PATTERNS

The following is a list of symbolic patterns for floor coverings, borders, textiles, and garden paving:

Symbol	Meaning
Tortoiseshell	Long life
Clouds	Wisdom and heavenly blessings
Rippling water	Wealth and the blessings of heaven
Coins	Wealth

NUMBERS

Paintings, calligraphy, and other decorative objects are often displayed in pairs in Chinese homes; it is believed that happiness comes in twos. However, as numbers have symbolic meanings, you may also arrange compositions containing specific numbers of objects, works of art, artifacts, rocks, and plants to add another subtly meaningful dimension to your space.

One symbolizes the beginning, the manifestation of the Boundless, the Supreme Ultimate, the fundamental unity of all things. It represents uniqueness, the ego, individuality, selfhood, self-assertion, self-reliance, distinction, rulership, and fame. It denotes simplicity and wholeness, as well as success and luck.

Two represents plus and minus, yang and yin, male and female, sun and moon, beginning and completion, mountain and valley, heaven and earth. It symbolizes the dualism of relative existence, or the relations of opposites, and as such denotes reflection, attraction, and the emotions of sympathy, love, and mutual caring. Because it unites the opposites in itself, it also denotes combination, creation, and productivity. It is traditionally considered to be a most lucky number.

Three symbolizes plurality, expansion, abundance, versatility, and success. It represents such triads as the Buddha, Dharma, Sangha; heaven, earth, and man; the sun, moon, and stars; water, fire, and wind; the three realms of existence (the lower world, our world, and the upper world); the past, present, and future; the three stages of life (childhood, maturity, and old age); the three virtues of kindness, simplicity, and humility; and the "three friends"—the plum tree, the pine, and the bamboo, so-called because they stay green in the winter. It also denotes the three ascending stages of energy, known in Chinese alchemy as *ching*, or generative force, *chi*, or vital force and *shen*, or spirit.

Four represents the wheel of the law, the cardinal points east, west, north, and south; the material universe; positive substance, realization, and stability. It symbolizes the four seasons and their corresponding flowers, the peony, lotus, chrysanthemum, and plum; the "four beauties"—music, fine food, poetry, and pleasant conversation; and the four plants known as "the four gentlemen"—the plum, orchid, bamboo, and chrysanthemum. Four combined with 8, 48, or 84, denotes prosperity.

Five, as the central number of one through nine, symbolizes balancing, pivoting, and transforming. It denotes the five elements; the five symbolic colors; the five directions—the four cardinal points plus the center; the five tastes—sweet for the element Earth, bitter for Metal, salty for Water, sour for Wood, and hot for Fire. It also denotes the five tones of the musical scale, and because it denotes the totality of the elements of the Taoist theory of nature, it represents fullness and all-inclusiveness.

Six represents the six auspicious spirits of the sun, the moon, lightning, wind, the mountains, and the rivers. It denotes the six relatives—father, mother, elder brother (or sister), younger brother (or sister), wife (or husband), and children. It symbolizes marriage, reciprocity, interaction of the spiritual and material dimensions, sympathy, love, peace, harmony, beauty, and sexual union, as well as art, music, and dance. It also denotes the six emotions of joyousness, anger, love, hate, delight, and sorrow.

Seven is a mysterious number. It signifies the seven ages, the seven planets, and the seven days of the week. It denotes completion, duration, and wisdom, and, as it is believed to take seven times seven, or forty-nine, days for the soul to pass from death to the wheel of rebirth, or from death to the deathless pure land, it denotes the renewal of life and immortality.

Eight symbolizes great luck and power. It represents the eight directions of space and the eight great solar days, the days during the year when the sun's rays are most powerful for the earth, those being the Winter Solstice, December 21 (or zero degrees Capricorn); the beginning of spring, February 4 (or fifteen degrees Aquarius); the Vernal Equinox, March 20 (or zero degrees Aries); the beginning of summer, May 5 (or fifteen degrees Taurus); the Summer Solstice, June 21 (or zero degrees Cancer); the beginning of autumn, August 7 (or fifteen degrees Leo); the Autumn Equinox, September 22 (or zero degrees Libra); and the beginning of winter, November 7 (or fifteen degrees Scorpio). It represents the eight trigrams of the *I Ching*, and, in their sixty-four combinations, the fullness of the interactions of yin and yang; and as it also represents the eight Taoist immortals, denotes long life and great wisdom.

Nine represents the nine heavens, and as such it denotes spirituality, vastness, distant voyages, prophetic dreams, extrasensory perception, long life, and great strength.

Ten is the number of fullness, or completeness. It symbolizes great wealth, longevity, and many offspring.

EXERCISES

1. Using the eight point method, choose an area of your life you want to con-
    centrate on. Choose, from the different symbolic decorations, what you feel
    will work best to activate and bless that area for you.

2. To bring forth the auspicious chi from one of your lucky stars, locate the cor-
    responding place for it in your home and then apply an appropriate form of
    symbolic decoration to it.

3. If you have a garden, choose a siting point and locate the direction of either
    your birth star or one of your lucky stars. Then plant one of the trees or flow-
    ers listed in this chapter for its symbolic meaning. If, for example, your birth
    star is 3 Wood, you might plant a peach tree to the east of your siting point.
    If you were born in the autumn, and your lucky star is 9 Fire, you could plant
    chrysanthemums to the south of your siting point. If you were born in the
    winter of a 4 Wood year, you could plant a plum tree to the southeast of your
    siting point.

TYING IT ALL TOGETHER

I would like to give you a few examples of various people with whom I have worked so that you can understand how the principles and theories I have discussed can be synthesized, and how feng shui can change lives dramatically as people become harmonized with their homes. Names have been changed to protect my clients' privacy. Note also that I have created reference charts for your use which can be found in the Appendices.

THE SMITH FAMILY

Sam and Susan lived with their children, Sally and Sean, in a suburban single-family home. Despite Sam and Susan's love for each other, serious problems were developing between them; their marriage was unraveling and in danger of coming apart. They were suffering serious financial losses, and the children showed increasing signs of unhappiness. Uncharacteristically, both were doing poorly in school and their teachers were becoming concerned.

First, note the Smith family birth dates. Sam was born on July 3, 1959, Susan on October 11, 1963, Sally on June 13, 1983, and Sean on May 5, 1985. The following is a chart of their personal data:

	SAM	SUSAN	SALLY	SEAN
SEASON OF BIRTH	Summer	Autumn	Summer	Summer
ELEMENT	Fire	Metal	Fire	Fire
BIRTH STAR	5 Earth	5 Earth	7 Metal	6 Metal
LUCKY STARS	2 Earth 6 Metal 8 Earth	2 Earth 7 Metal 8 Earth	2 Earth 6 Metal	7 Metal 8 Earth

Note that Sam, Sally, and Sean were all born during the summer, or Fire season, but Susan was born during the autumn, or Metal season.

Sam's birth star is 5 Earth and his lucky stars are 2 Earth, 6 Metal, and 8 Earth. Susan's birth star is also 5 Earth and her lucky stars are 2 Earth, 7 Metal, and 8 Earth. Sally's birth star is 7 Metal and her lucky stars are 2 Earth and 6 Metal. Sean's birth star is 6 Metal and his lucky stars are 7 Metal and 8 Earth.

Interestingly, Sam and Susan both have the same birth star, 5 Earth, and share 2 and 8 Earth Stars as their lucky stars. Sally shares lucky star 2 Earth with both her father and mother, and Sean shares lucky star 8 Earth with both parents.

Judging from their birth stars, Sam and Susan are both attracted to business and finance and are capable of hard work. But both are very stubborn. In fact, it was largely due to their stubbornness that their marriage was in trouble. As both were born under 5 Earth, they had given in to their tendencies to become suspicious and quarrelsome.

I looked for more information about negative conditions in their home and I found the following clues, represented in figure 187.

The Smiths' house needed to be decorated in a cheerful but orderly fashion to suit the seasons of their births, summer and autumn. In reality, however, their home was cluttered and decorated with somber colors, which indicated signs of trouble in their lives.

As I proceeded through the rooms of the house, I noted further signs of dis-

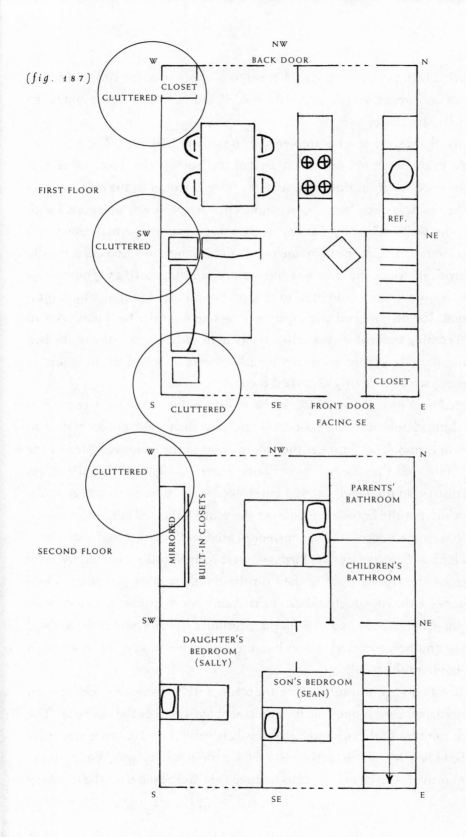

(fig. 187)

FIRST FLOOR

SECOND FLOOR

tress. In the kitchen, the stove, or Fire element, was opposed to the sink and refrigerator, or Water element, which, as you may recall, indicates opposition and fighting between husband and wife.

Upstairs, there were several problems in the master bedroom. The bedroom was situated in the west and northwest area of the house, which was an area of negative chi since the front door and stairway were oriented to the southeast. In addition, the bed was also absorbing negative chi because it was positioned with its head to the wall backed by the two bathrooms. One of the bathrooms was attached to the bedroom at the marriage point, and was not only depleting the chi associated with marriage but also was linking the Smiths' marriage symbolically with waste. Moreover, the plumbing in this bathroom was leaking, which indicated financial losses. The bed was positioned in line with the bedroom door so that the chi coming in the door cut across the bed. In addition, the foot of the bed was pointing directly at a series of full-length mirrors attached to the doors of built-in closets, which seriously disturbed the couple's rest.

Cluttered conditions were found at the money point in the west corners of the house, both downstairs and upstairs, indicating financial troubles linked to poor communication. The clutter at the family point in the southwest area of the downstairs indicated that Susan was suffering from anxiety and that there was worry and distress in the family around unresolved issues of support and nourishment. The clutter at the knowledge point in the south indicated confusion associated with love; something was being misrepresented and/or concealed.

If you look at Sam and Susan's birth star as it relates to the front doorway of their house, an interesting light is shed on the Smith family's problems. Their doorway faces southeast, which indicates that Sam's good fortune is linked to his fidelity to the family. (See chapter 8 on door fortunes.) However, Susan doubted Sam's fidelity and her suspicions about him created an animosity that resulted in tension throughout the family.

Thus, the first step in resolving the problems and balancing the chi of their house was to balance everyone's birth star element with that of the doorway. The birth star element for both Sam and Susan was Earth and the birth star element for Sally and Sean was Metal. Since the element for the doorway was Wood, it was necessary to provide the Fire element to balance Sam and Susan with the doorway and introduce the Water element to balance Sally and Sean with the doorway. This was easily done by putting a small area rug in front of the door that included a light blue color for Wood, dark blue for Water, and a plum color for Fire.

The Smiths' next step was to sort out their cluttered areas and repair the plumbing in the bathroom upstairs.

The kitchen problem was solved by placing a light blue floor mat between the stove and sink, which introduced Wood to bring the Fire and Water elements into harmony and reduce Sam and Susan's fighting.

Upstairs in the master bedroom, a full-length mirror was placed on the outside of the bathroom door to transform the negative chi coming into the bedroom from the bathroom. The mirrors were removed from the doors of the built-in closets to relax the chi in the bedroom. The built-in closets and the bed were switched to the opposite walls, as shown in figure 188. This put the bed in a more restful area, which was out of the way of the bedroom door.

(fig. 188)

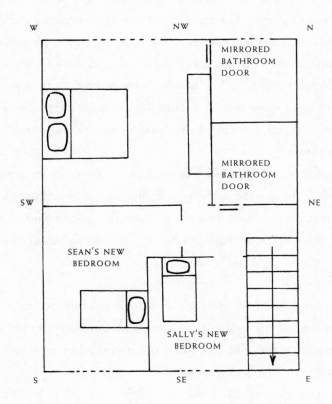

203

A full-length mirror was placed on the outside of the children's bathroom door to transform the negative chi that came in a direct line from the bathroom into Sean's bedroom.

In addition, I recommended that Sally and Sean exchange bedrooms, as it would allow them to have their beds aligned to their lucky stars, as shown in figure 188. Sean's bed aligned to the northeast was only possible in the bedroom used by Sally, and Sally's bed aligned to the northwest was only possible in the bedroom used by Sean.

The chi of the house also needed to be balanced with colors. The entire home was brightened with cheerful displays of flowers and works of art, so that Fire energy would be stimulated for Sam, Sally, and Sean. The dining room, originally tan and brown, was decorated with white and blue. The cooking area of the kitchen, originally white, was decorated with red hues. The master bedroom, originally white, tan, and ocher, was decorated with cream and blue.

Finally, a new area needed to be created and arranged so that it would symbolically support the marriage. The north quadrant, the eating area in the kitchen, was chosen because it was the marriage point of the house. A picture of wild geese, symbolizing conjugal fidelity, was hung there, and the whole area was made to feel comfortable and inviting. The whole room received a thorough cleaning, white lace curtains were hung over the window, and an attractive new table with two new chairs was placed in front of the window so that Sam and Susan might spend some quiet time together.

The Smith family life improved. Sam and Susan spent more time with each other; they loved their special place at the marriage point. Susan's suspicions regarding Sam's infidelity faded. The children were happier and more relaxed. They loved their new bedrooms and, last heard, were doing better at school.

JENNIFER LEE

Jennifer Lee was a single woman, aged 36, who lived in a one-bedroom apartment. Although Jennifer was doing well in her career and was quite active, socially she was lonely and discontented. She had been disappointed in love and was beginning to despair, believing she would never get married.

Jennifer was born on April 24, 1958. Her birth star is 9 Fire and her lucky star is 4 Wood. Born in the spring, or Wood season, of a 9 birth star year, she is naturally optimistic and youthful, warmhearted and sunny, and full of creative ideas and plans.

Combining the correspondences of Jennifer's birth star (9 Fire), season of birth (spring), yin physical constitution, and her graphic arts career, also yin, I deduced that her home should be brightly and cheerfully decorated with rectangular and square shapes, colorful displays of flowers and/or works of art, and the colors of Wood, Fire, and Earth (light blues and greens, reds and purples, and gold). Her lucky star, 4 Wood, favored green. It was also important that Jennifer have a relatively quiet area to use as a study and library.

Jennifer's apartment has the following configuration of rooms:

(fig. 189)

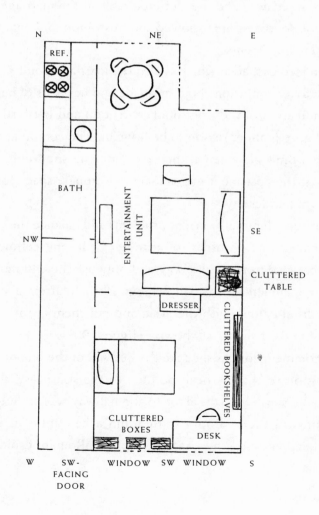

There were two entrances to Jennifer's bedroom, one from the hallway and one from the living room. This meant that the eight points of her room could be read in two different ways, depending on which door was more frequently used. Since Jennifer had combined her bedroom with her work space, she was accustomed to using the entrance from the hallway. This not only caused her bedroom to become too active and exposed to the outside world, but it also put her desk at the marriage point of the room, indicating that she was crowding out her love life with her work.

In addition, shelves, cluttered with loose papers and books in the south area facing the bed, indicated that she was experiencing anxiety and confusion about love. More boxes filled with loose papers in the southwest area further reflected her feelings of insecurity, and the cluttered table at the marriage point of her living room in the southeast area showed the frustration and anger associated with her romantic entanglements.

The depressed east area, which is also the marriage point of the entire apartment, indicated her confusion about marriage and her fears of being trapped.

The combination of the front door's direction and her birth star were good, however, and gave Jennifer reason to be hopeful. The combination indicated that if she bided her time and acted at the right moment, she would have a fortuitous marriage. Thus, the apartment was actually a fortunate space for her in allowing her to transform her destiny.

To help resolve Jennifer's current problems and balance the chi of her home, I first recommended that, in order to make her bedroom feel more secluded, she close off its entrance from the hallway and only use the entrance from the living room. I then recommended that she remove all the clutter, take the bookshelves out of the bedroom along with the desk, and put them at the back of the living room area and in the hallway, as shown in figure 190.

I also recommended that she take the bed out of the line of her doorway and move its position so that its head pointed to the southeast, the direction of 4 Wood, her lucky star. Once the door to the hallway was sealed, the positions of the eight points in the bedroom shifted and a new intimate seating area was arranged at her bedroom's new marriage point. Romantic pictures were hung there.

(fig. 190)

T
Y
I
N
G

I
T

A
L
L

T
O
G
E
T
H
E
R

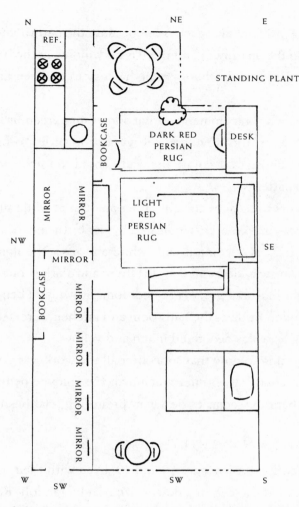

The back area of the living room was set up as a work space. Her desk was positioned so that she would have the window to her left instead of directly in front of her as it had been in the bedroom. To help define the work space and the social area of the living room, two Persian rugs of varying hues of red were introduced. The brighter one was placed in the social area, while the darker one was placed in the work space to emphasize the yin nature of her work.

The depressed east area between the living room and the dining area was resolved by hanging curtains with patterns of green and rose. A standing plant placed at the east corner also served to resolve the depressed area while giving the dining area added definition.

A full-length mirror was hung on the outside of the bathroom door, and mirrors were hung inside to face each other because the bathroom door is visible from the entrance to the apartment and there is no window in the bathroom. A series of full-length mirrors was also hung in the hallway to compensate for its length and stuffy feeling.

In the kitchen, I recommended that something green or light blue be placed in the area between the stove and refrigerator in order to harmonize their elements. Jennifer chose to decorate the wall behind the stove with Dutch tiles that had light blue patterns.

Using colors to balance the chi of her apartment while simultaneously incorporating her personal colors, as indicated by her birth and lucky stars, the hallway, originally white, was decorated with white and rose; the living room, originally blue and brown, was decorated in brighter and darker hues of red with some touches of light blue and green; the bedroom, brown and beige, was decorated in cream color and light blue; the bathroom and kitchen were decorated all in white; and the dining area was decorated in tan and yellow.

It is interesting to note that soon after all the work was done and the position of her bed was changed, Jennifer met a man she enjoyed being with and was able to establish what now seems to be a very promising relationship.

THE BROWN FAMILY

Robert and Carolyn Brown, ages 50 and 49, lived with their son, Michael, age 14, and daughter, Linda, age 9, in a downtown Manhattan loft. Robert was successful in business and was generally happy with his life. Carolyn, on the other hand, was in a state of confusion and flux, trying to decide whether to continue being a full-time mother and housewife or embark on a new career. Michael was generally happy. He had many friends and was doing well in school. Linda, although she was doing well in school, was a sensitive child and easily distressed.

Robert's date of birth was August 12, 1944, and Carolyn's was October 13, 1945. Thus, both parents were born during the autumn, or Metal season. Michael was born March 1, 1980, and Linda, February 10, 1985, which means that both children were born during the spring, or Wood season.

The Brown family's stars are as follows: Robert's birth star is 2 Earth and his

lucky stars are 6 Metal, 7 Metal, and 8 Earth. Carolyn's birth star is 5 Earth and her lucky stars are 2 Earth, 7 Metal, and 8 Earth. Like his father, Michael's birth star is 2 Earth and his lucky stars are 5 Earth, 6 Metal, 7 Metal, 8 Earth, and 9 Fire. Linda's birth star is 9 Fire and her lucky stars are 3 Wood and 4 Wood.

The following is a chart of the Brown family's personal data:

	ROBERT	CAROLYN	MICHAEL	LINDA
SEASON OF BIRTH	Autumn	Autumn	Spring	Spring
ELEMENT	Metal	Metal	Wood	Wood
BIRTH STAR	2 Earth	5 Earth	2 Earth	9 Fire
LUCKY STARS	6 Metal	2 Earth	5 Earth	3 Wood
	7 Metal	7 Metal	6 Metal	4 Wood
	8 Earth	8 Earth	7 Metal	
			8 Earth	
			9 Fire	

Michael had more in common with his parents, especially his father, than with Linda, even though he and Linda were born in the same season. The father, mother, and son were all West types, born under Earth stars, and they all had 7 Metal and 8 Metal as their lucky stars. In contrast, Linda was an East type and she shared no lucky stars with the others. She was completely different and therefore was of special interest.

The birth stars of Michael and his parents were in harmony with the west-facing door, but Linda's birth star was out of harmony with the door.

Their fortunes, as derived from the combinations of their birth stars with the compass direction of the doorway, revealed that Robert and Michael were in a harmonious and lucky place, that Carolyn needed to cultivate independent thinking if she was to attain any of her own goals, and that Linda was faced with hardships and challenges. I determined, therefore, that I would have to concentrate on Carolyn and Linda's situations and balance the space more to their advantage.

Combining everyone's birth stars with their seasons revealed that the Brown home should be very comfortable yet orderly. It should be warmly decorated with square shapes, beautiful displays of flowers and works of art, and with the colors of Earth and Fire, or yellows and reds, where possible. It also should provide the children with ample space for studying and for creative activities. Looking at their home as shown in figure 191, the following indications were found:

(*fig. 191*)

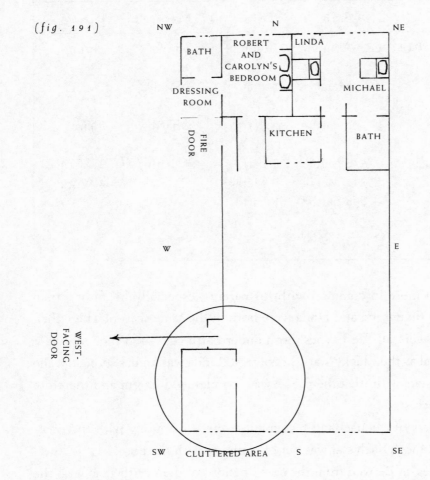

The bedrooms were situated at the back end of the loft and their windows opened on an air shaft. The bedrooms were dark and oppressive and, to make matters worse, the parents' bedroom was painted dark blue.

The cluttered condition of the parents' bedroom in the north and northwest areas of the loft hinted at some of the underlying causes of Carolyn's difficulties in defining her career goals. She was concealing her aims from herself because of her fears of change or of losing control of the life she had. The clutter in the southwest area also showed her deep worry over her confused creative drives. The exaggerations of the northwest and southwest areas (symbolizing the father and mother respectively) show both Robert and Carolyn as very strong and willful. They further hint that Carolyn was afraid that if she did assert her independence and change the family's status quo, she and Robert would come into opposition.

In addition to difficulties indicated by the cluttered areas, everyone's bed was in the wrong position. Michael's and his parents' beds were aligned to the east and were out of harmony with their birth and lucky stars. Linda's bed was in a most unfortunate long, narrow space, with its head at one wall and its foot at the other.

To remedy these problems, and to balance the chi of the space with colors, the following steps were taken, as shown in figure 192.

(*fig. 192*)

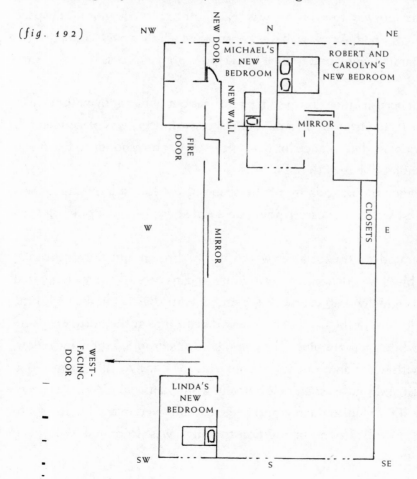

Each person's bed was realigned to his or her lucky star. Linda was given the southwest room and her bed was positioned so that she would be able to sleep with her head pointing east. The clutter that had been in the southwest corner was eliminated and new closets were built in the eastern section of the loft. Then, the wall that divided Linda's original space from Michael's was taken down. The enlarged room was assigned to Robert and Carolyn, and their bed was positioned so they would be able to sleep with their heads pointing west, the direction of 7 Metal, one of their lucky stars. A mirrored wall was constructed and placed in the entrance to their bedroom as a barrier to protect them from intrusions and to stop the chi from coming directly into the bedroom and cutting across their bed. The original space of the parents' bedroom became Michael's bedroom, and his bed was positioned so that his head pointed south, the direction of his lucky star, 9 Fire. The original doorway to his room was sealed off to provide more wall space and accommodate his bed. A new wall was constructed with a new door to give his room a more separate feeling and to give Linda more private access to the adjoining bathroom.

In addition, because Linda's birth star, 9 Fire, was out of harmony with the element of the west-facing front door, a picture of yellow flowers was placed next to the door to provide needed balance for her, since yellow corresponds to Earth and mitigates the conflict of Fire with Metal.

To help balance the irregularity of the shape of the loft, a large mirror was placed on the west wall at the career point, an auspicious place, considering Carolyn's dilemma.

The exaggerated northwest area, which is a bathroom and dressing room, originally dark blue, was decorated with white and navy, and the exaggerated southwest area, originally drab yellow, was painted white. Balancing the chi of the space with the element of the front door, the two bedrooms at the north end were decorated with white and light blue. The parents' new bedroom, originally yellow, was decorated with white and touches of gold to favor Carolyn. The main room, because of its east and southeast areas, originally white, tan, and green, was decorated with ivory, light blue, and navy, and beige curtains were placed at the south windows. Linda's new bedroom, in addition to white, was decorated with green accents to accommodate her lucky star, 4 Wood. Purple accents were used in Michael's new room to accommodate his lucky star, 9 Fire.

Soon after the changes were made, Carolyn was able to make the decision to take up interior designing as her career, something she had always wanted to do. Linda, who was thrilled with her new bedroom, became much happier and began dancing lessons. Michael was very pleased with his new bedroom, and Robert was glad to see the positive changes in the lives of his wife and daughter.

BILL

A writer and teacher, Bill is a bachelor, age 32, who lives by himself in a small one-bedroom apartment. He called me because he was experiencing insomnia, writer's block, and financial difficulties. He was also grieving over a failed affair and was questioning his ability to have a meaningful relationship with a woman.

Born on May 10, 1963, Bill's birth star is 1 Water and his lucky stars are 6 Metal and 7 Metal. Born in the summer, or Fire season, of a 1 Water year, Bill is ambitious, hardworking, talented, intensely emotional, desirous of attention, and attracted to love relationships. At the same time, he is self-protective and secretive.

The combination of Bill's birth star and season with his yang physical constitution and his yin career in teaching and writing revealed that his home should be painted in yin hues and decorated with round, flowing shapes and patterns, beautiful displays of flowers and/or works of art, and the colors of Water and Metal, or black, white (for his lucky star 6 Metal), and light red (for his lucky star 7 Metal).

The condition of Bill's apartment, shown in figure 193, provided the following information:

(*fig. 193*)

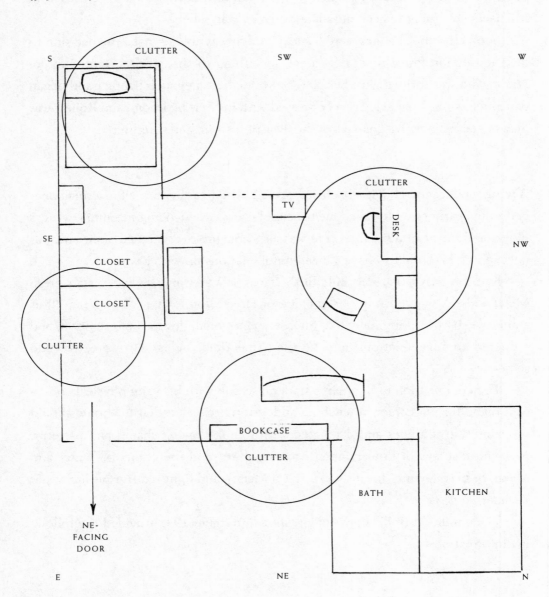

Clutter in the east area at the knowledge point in front of the entrance showed that Bill was feeling confused and indecisive, and that he had many obstacles in his path. The cluttered bookcase in the northeast area at the career point indicated he was concerned that he did not know enough to be successful in his career. Clutter around his desk in the west area at the marriage point showed that his grief over the failure of a relationship and unwillingness to let go were involved with his writer's block. There was a clutter of papers and boxes underneath his king-sized bed, which was jammed up against the window and against the two walls of the small room to the south at the exaggerated money point. All of this showed that his tendency to live beyond his means and incur debts was related to his emotional upsets and troubled love affairs.

It was plain to see that his bed cramped his chi and exposed him to potential danger. The cold draft from the window also caused him to feel quite vulnerable.

The exaggerated north area was at the friends point and revealed the fears and congested emotions involved with Bill's social life. The opposition of the north area (Water) and south area (Fire) revealed conflict. A simple remedy was required: the north area, which included the kitchen and bathroom, was decorated with hues of green and blue, the colors of Wood, to balance the exaggerated Water element. The small room in the south area was painted beige, the color of Earth, to balance the exaggerated Fire element.

The front door of Bill's apartment faced northeast. The combination of the doorway with Bill's birth star (1 Water) indicated that this was a lonely place for him, but that if he were willing to live simply and be adaptable and patient, he would eventually be successful.

To help resolve Bill's problems and balance the chi of his apartment, all the clutter was sorted out and cleared away. The bookcase at the career point was neatly arranged, with a special focus placed on those books he found most interesting and relevant to his career.

The king-sized bed was taken out of the small room and a Murphy bed installed at the northwest wall, as shown in figure 194, so that when Bill slept there, his head would point in the direction of his lucky star, 6 Metal, and he would have plenty of space around him. A screen was introduced so that the bed was concealed from the front door and a foyer area could be delineated.

The small room to the south was entirely cleared out and converted into a study. The desk was moved out of the west corner of the main room and repositioned so that when Bill sat there he would have command of the door and have the window on his left side, as he is right-handed. The bathroom had no window.

(fig. 194)

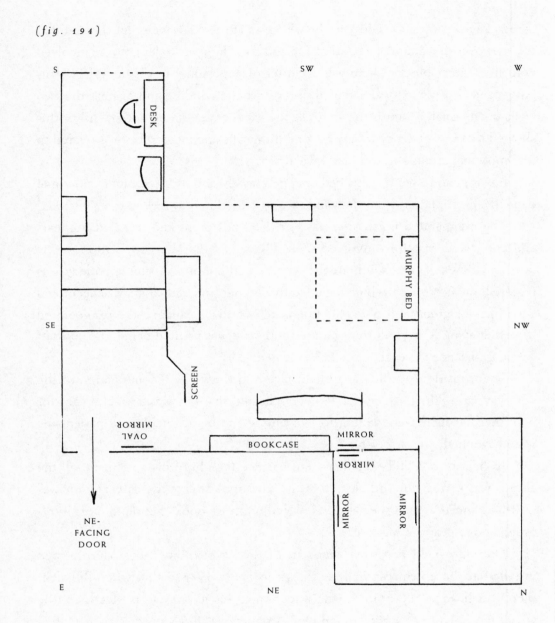

Mirrors were installed opposite each other on the walls so that they would reflect each other and activate the chi.

The main room, originally white and beige, was not in need of any special balancing with the Earth element of the front door, but was decorated in black, cream, and light red, the colors of Bill's birth and lucky stars. An oval mirror, corresponding to the element Metal, was hung on the wall next to the front door to balance the Water element of Bill's birth star with the Earth element of his front door. The newly created foyer in the east quadrant of Bill's apartment was decorated with subdued colors of Fire, or reds and purples to harmonize with the doorway. White curtains were hung at the window in Bill's new study to accommodate his lucky star, 6 Metal.

When all the changes were made, Bill felt much better. He was able to resolve his grief and take a new and more conscientious interest in his social life. This enabled him to renew his interest in his work, stop living beyond his means, overcome his writer's block, and recuperate from his insomnia. He soon was busy with a new creative project and was thoroughly enjoying it.

FINDING A NEW HOME AND MAKING ALTERATIONS

Finding a new home always marks a turning point in life. Sorting things out, throwing away what is no longer useful, packing up, moving out of the old place, and moving into the new place naturally helps you resolve the past and make decisions for your future.

The time of your move is important and will have either positive or negative effects on your health, career, finances, and relationships. Before you actually begin your move, spend some time reviewing all that you have accomplished from the past to the present, and clarify your future plans as best you can. If you move for positive reasons, and to a good place in a good time, good fortune will follow. If you move under difficult circumstances, but to a good place in a good time, your luck will change for the better. If, however, you move under difficult circumstances to a bad place in a bad time, you will be jumping from the frying pan into the fire.

There are many people who unwittingly move to places that cause adverse conditions to develop in their lives, or who move to places that magnify adverse conditions already existing. For example, a family moved into a house that brought them into serious financial difficulties, or a couple divorced after they moved into a house in which the prior owners divorced, as did the owners before them. A woman, suffering from extreme nervousness and digestive problems—disorders associated with unbalanced Earth—found her symptoms exacerbated when she moved into an apartment, the basic shape of which is shown in figure 195.

(fig. 195)

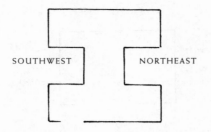

SOUTHWEST   NORTHEAST

In addition to having its southwest and northeast areas depressed and its middle pinched, this shape resembles the Chinese character *kung*, meaning labor. It is considered an unlucky shape, and those who live in such a space will find themselves overburdened in life.

If you decide to move, consider the following guidelines before you commit:

1. You should feel invigorated and uplifted in the space you choose.

2. If you have found a place you like, try to investigate its history and that of its prior tenants. Old places have happy or sad memories, however subtle, that can affect you for good or ill. All places, for that matter, as they have shapes, or energy patterns, have personalities that influence your life and affairs. It is necessary, therefore, to be aware of how you feel about a place. If you really love it, it will probably be auspicious for you. But if you don't have a positive reaction, don't rationalize what you think are its good points. Don't take it.

3. If you are looking at a house in the country, take note of the land's features. A site that is exposed on all sides, with neither hills, a body of water, nor trees to protect it, or conversely, a site on a hilltop or an unusually windy place, holds neither chi nor money and is therefore undesirable. A site that is hemmed in or sunken, where the air does not freely circulate, receives sha and causes illness, which is also undesirable. It is not a good idea to have a house positioned directly in line with a roadway, for example, at a T- or Y-junction, or so that water runs directly and visibly toward or away from the main entrance. Also, beware of railroad tracks, telephone and electric wires, and tower antennas that are distinctly visible from your doors or windows.

4. The best site for a house is one that sits amid hills and/or trees as if it were seated in an armchair. Hills and trees should rise up behind and to the left and right of the site.

(fig. 196)

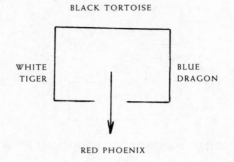

BLACK TORTOISE

WHITE
TIGER

BLUE
DRAGON

RED PHOENIX

The back, left, front, and right sides are characteristically named the Black Tortoise, the Blue Dragon, the Red Phoenix, and the White Tiger, respectively. As shown in figure 196, if you stand at the front door and look out of your house, the Black Tortoise will be at your back, the Blue Dragon will be at your left, the Red Phoenix will be in front of you, and the White Tiger will be at your right.

Ideally, the Black Tortoise and Blue Dragon should rise up higher than the White Tiger, and Red Phoenix should not rise up at all, but should be an interesting object or land formation off in the distance. If the White Tiger and Blue Dragon are equal, the situation is still good. The Blue Dragon gives life and the White Tiger takes life, so if the White Tiger rises up above the Blue Dragon and dominates the site, the situation will not be fortuitous.

If the house has land rising up in front so that you have to climb a hill when leaving, serious blockage may result. An even more negative aspect suggesting defenselessness occurs if the land falls away behind your house.

A house on elevated ground with hills rising up behind it and with a lake or winding river in front of it is the most favorably positioned. It is most auspicious to have a river or stream flowing from the Tiger side to the Dragon side.

If a house is built on open flat land, you can create the chi of the Black Tortoise, Blue Dragon, and White Tiger by planting trees to screen the house and property.

5. A house should be at a comfortable distance from the road, neither too near nor too far from it. There should also be trees or bushes to screen the house from the road, but they must not obstruct or crowd the doors or windows.

6. The best plots are those which are well balanced and have boundaries that conform to the natural features of the land. A triangular plot is least desirable, because it is associated with Fire. To mitigate the triangle's negative aspect, trees and bushes should be planted to create wooded areas that will camouflage and blur the corners, as illustrated in figure 197. In a similar manner, a plot with an unusual or irregular shape can be treated with trees and gardens, as suggested by figure 198.

(fig. 197)

(fig. 198)

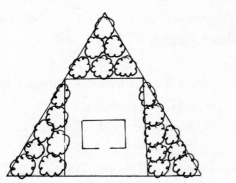

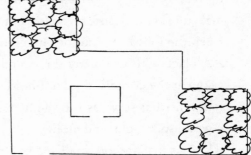

7. If you are looking at an apartment in town, always take note of the neighborhood or general surroundings. Note whether the apartment building is situated comfortably among the surrounding buildings and whether it feels open or cramped. Note whether the building is in harmony with the surrounding buildings, or if it towers above them and oppresses their chi, or if they tower above it to oppress its chi.

8. Compare the elements of the building by its overall shape and color to the shapes and colors of the surrounding buildings. Are the elements of the building in harmony with the elements of the surrounding buildings or not? Disharmony between the elements of the different buildings will generate sha in the environment, which will cause distressing conditions to develop in the lives of the people who reside there.

    Watch for other sources of sha, such as sharp protrusions, rooftops, or corners of buildings pointing directly at the windows of the apartment in question.

9. Note the condition of the apartment's structural features—the plumbing,

heating system, wiring, the floor, walls, and layout of the rooms. Is the apartment soundproof or are the walls too thin?

10. Does the apartment face the street corner or the middle of the block? An apartment that faces the corner is more exposed, and therefore yang, whereas one that faces the middle of the block is yin. An apartment on a high floor is yang, whereas an apartment on a low floor is yin. An apartment that faces a busy avenue is yang, and an apartment that faces a quiet street is yin. An apartment that faces the front of the building is yang, and an apartment that faces the back is yin. According to your personal data list, if your physical makeup is yang, choose an apartment that is yin. Conversely, if your physical makeup is yin, choose an apartment that is yang.

Keep the following cautions in mind:

- A place with too many doors and windows, especially with windows that join at the corners, does not hold in chi and is not peaceful.
- Rooms that serve as thoroughfares offer no privacy and will cause you to waste space, chi, and money.
- Rooms that are too small and confining are oppressive and will cause you to feel hemmed in and irritable.
- It is bad feng shui to have a bathroom facing the entrance to the apartment, or to have one that is located in the middle of the apartment or that opens onto the kitchen or another bathroom.
- It is bad feng shui to have a bedroom facing the entrance to the apartment, or to have a bedroom that opens onto another bedroom, or to the kitchen.

MAKING ALTERATIONS

Think carefully before you decide to change the shape of your house. Any addition to a house will change the balance of its chi. An addition that creates an irregular shape, unless integrated in a more comprehensive design involving landscapes and gardens, will only play havoc with the chi of the house and the fortunes of its occupants.

Conversely, an addition can be made advantageously that will balance an irregularly shaped house, as suggested in figure 199:

(fig. 199)

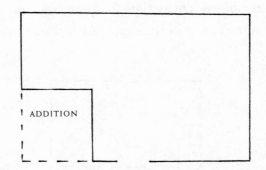

It is generally better to extend the breadth of the house by wings, as shown in figure 200, than to extend its depth, as shown in figure 201:

(fig. 200)   *(fig. 201)*

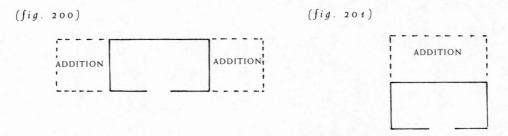

Be cautious about moving the front door. The following story will illustrate the point.

CATHERINE

Some time ago, I went to work on a house that had been undergoing rather extensive alterations. Catherine, its owner, was the designer. Never having liked the front door opening into the kitchen, she moved it to the side of the house, as shown in figure 202, and constructed a little vestibule. She also pulled out a supporting ceiling, which seriously weakened the entire structure.

Observing that Catherine had moved the doorway to the Tiger side of the house, I asked her if she had any accidents since doing so. She answered that recently she had had a car accident and injured her back.

To help mitigate the trouble Catherine had caused herself, I first recommended that she put back the supporting ceiling. Then, because the house is quite small and shallow, I recommended that she mirror the entire inside wall of the Tiger side, shown in figure 203. She chose a dark, smoky mirror. As indicated by the dotted lines, the mirror created the illusions of extension and symmetry, and put the doorway at the center of the space rather than at its edge.

(fig. 202)

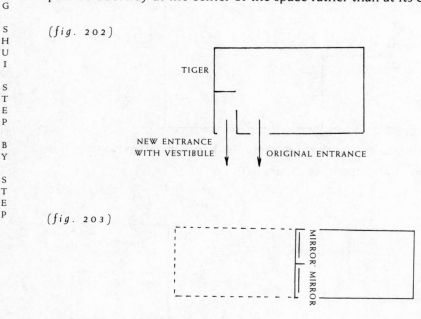

(fig. 203)

Next, because Catherine was interested in constructing a garden behind the house with a studio and pond, I recommended that she bring a stream of water around the Tiger side from behind the house, as shown in figure 204. This would neutralize the adverse influence of the Tiger and create an auspicious Water Dragon around the house to give her life-supportive chi.

When all of these changes and alterations were completed, the chi of the house was transformed. Not only was there now a beautiful garden in the back, but there was a beautiful feeling in the house. It made Catherine feel very happy and secure and, as she was able to relax and enjoy her new environment, her health began to improve.

(fig. 204)

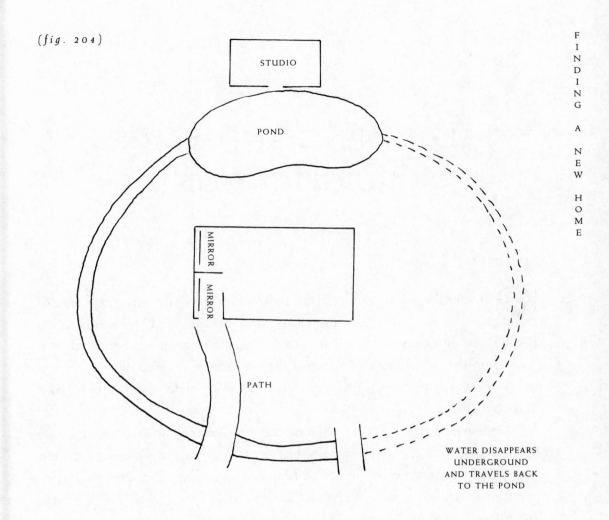

STUDIO

POND

MIRROR

MIRROR

PATH

WATER DISAPPEARS
UNDERGROUND
AND TRAVELS BACK
TO THE POND

DIVINING AND SPACE PURIFICATION

Divining is an art of communicating with the earth's energies, a way of bridging intuitive knowledge and rational thought, or of translating natural psychic responses into useful information. The ability to divine is natural; it is something that we all have. The art of divining can be learned quite easily—it only requires some practice. You may wish to try it. If you do, it will enhance your feng shui practice.

Divining, or dowsing, is a technique that employs the mind's natural aptitude for detecting what cannot be perceived by the five senses and the intellect. It is a way of reading intuitive responses to find anything at any distance, height, or depth. It is used to locate underground streams, to analyze ground, soil, and rock conditions, and to find such things as sunken wells, ruins, underground caves, tunnels, drains, cables, and so on. It can also be used to locate pipes, electrical wiring, and anything else that is hidden behind walls.

Too often, subterranean stresses that cause illnesses and other dire conditions elude observation. You may have heard of people who fall ill soon after moving into a building in which many of the tenants are ill. There are also stories of people who, after moving their business from one building to another, watch their business fail. I once worked with a food shop that had the heaviest and most exhausting energy of any place I had ever seen. It was also frequently robbed. When I dowsed the shop, I found a noxious ray running through the building. Having found the source of the shop's woes, I was able to cure it by neutralizing the ray.

Your body always responds to subtle environmental conditions, as well as to qualities, levels, and frequencies of energy from below ground. Two actions must be taken so that you can translate these subtle bodily responses into practical information that you can use to transform negative conditions into positive ones. The first is the actual process of dowsing; the second is asking relevant questions.

THE METHODS

Feng shui uses both deviceless dowsing and dowsing with various instruments, including the pendulum.

Deviceless dowsing is a basic skill for feng shui. It is the ability to be aware of what your body feels in any space. In this method, your body becomes the dowsing instrument. Start by noting your body's ordinary, everyday state. This is its neutral position. Then, note how it feels in different spaces. With practice, you will note that you feel more energized in one space while, in another, you will feel more depleted. You may even feel ill in some places.

The method of deviceless dowsing can be refined so that it is possible to detect specific conditions of energy through the hands and feet. The essential technique is to know what to ask and to trust your intuitive response. To illustrate the point, I was walking about in the basement of a client's house when it occurred to me that there might be a problem connected to water. I began slowly pacing back and forth across the floor, searching, every couple of steps silently asking whether there was water there, or there, or there. After covering the entire area, I told the owner of the house that water was coming up from under the basement in two very specific places, and that the cellar would probably be flooded before long. The owner said that it was impossible. Two weeks later, however, I received a phone call. Water was coming up through the basement floor in exactly those two areas.

The ability to dowse through the hands, which is related to the ability to see, or sense auras, can become highly developed. Many people who practice *chi kung* (a Chinese system of exercises) or yoga have this skill. It can be cultivated easily through exercises such as the following:

Hold your open hands in front of an object such as a plant, a tree, or a rock;

then move closer and farther away from it to get a sense of its energy field. Note subtle differences of feeling that you get from different sorts of objects. You can apply the method to walls and floors to find where the energy is stronger and weaker, more positive and more negative. You can also refine it to find out where streams of water and lines of electromagnetic energy run below the ground.

A somewhat mechanical, but very effective, technique of divining with the hands can be done as follows:

Stand up straight, in a relaxed and balanced posture. Hold out your hands, palms down, your forearms parallel to the ground, upper arms hanging down freely, and shoulders relaxed. Walk slowly toward the object of your search. When you approach it, your hands and forearms will rise up a few inches. When you move past it, your hands and forearms will return to their original position.

An alternative method may feel more natural to you. It is the same as the above except that as you approach the object of your search, your hands will go down, and as you leave it, they will rise back to their original position. Whichever method you use is entirely a matter of personal preference. Once you make your choice, however, stay with it.

To illustrate the technique, suppose you want to find a stream of water running somewhere underneath your backyard, lawn, or field. Assume the search, or original, position. Proceed to walk in a snake-like path, back and forth across the entire area, marking wherever your hands rise or fall. Connect all the points you marked and you will see the outline of the stream.

THE PENDULUM

For fine precision, many diviners prefer to work with a pendulum.

When you begin to experiment with a pendulum, you will notice that the shorter the string length, the faster it swings and rotates. According to your preference, the string length can be anywhere from two to seven inches.

The technique for using the pendulum is quite simple. First it is necessary to establish how you and the pendulum work together. Notice how the pendulum feels when it hangs motionless, when it swings forward and back, side to side and diagonally, and when it rotates clockwise and counterclockwise.

Holding its string or chain between your thumb and index finger, let the pendulum hang motionless. Then say, "Show me my starting position." At this point it will either remain motionless or begin to swing back and forth. Repeat it a few times. You should get the same response. If you get different responses, decide on one of them by saying, "This one is my starting position." Then say, "Show me yes. What is yes?" It will swing back and forth or from side to side, or it will rotate either clockwise or counterclockwise. After this, say, "Show me no. What is no?" If it swung back and forth for yes, it will swing from side to side for no. If it rotated for yes, it will also rotate, but in the opposite direction, for no. Finally, you need to say, "Show me out of line. What is out of line?" It will do any number of things. It might stay at starting position or swing diagonally. Watch it carefully to establish its signal. You will always get the "out of line" response when your line of questioning is either confused, too vague, or drifting off course.

You should go through all these initial steps of establishing your code—or system of answers—for every different pendulum you get and use. Each pendulum is unique, and each pendulum's responses can and do vary. You may find that you prefer to work with one over another.

All questions you put to the pendulum must be concise and simple. They must be posed so that the answers will be either yes or no. Complex questions must be analyzed and broken down into simple questions.

You can either organize your line of questioning from general to specific, letting the answer to one question serve as the basis of the next, or you can cut through to the heart of the matter by letting your intuition guide you.

Whichever method of questioning you decide to use, however, you have to know what to ask. This means that you have to be conversant with the elements of your subject of interest. If you are interested in applying pendulum dowsing to horticulture, for instance, you will need a working knowledge of plants and soil culture to formulate proper questions. If you are interested in detecting and curing underground sha, read on.

There is a protocol to pendulum dowsing that should always be used. Before opening a line of questioning, it is necessary to ask the pendulum, "May I explore this?" or "May I search for this?" and so on. If you get a no answer, don't pursue it. Wait for a more propitious time to ask. The most important key to divining is trust.

The following guidelines will help you develop the skill:

1. Divining is seeking. Your curiosity is what guides it.
2. The answers come spontaneously. Keep the rational process from intercepting them. Let them happen.
3. There must be a genuine desire to know the truth.
4. Be adventurous and probing.
5. Have confidence that you can do it.
6. Be open-minded. Preconceptions can put you in a dreamland or close you out altogether.

There are seven obstacles to accurate divining. The first is having doubts that it works; the second is having doubts that you can do it; the third is lack of proper attention; the fourth is lack of interest in the matter of your search; the fifth is lack of knowledge about the matter of your search, or not knowing what to ask; the sixth is wishful thinking, or letting what you want to see override the truth; the seventh is being afraid of finding out the truth.

Dowsing for Underground Sha

If you enter or live in a place that feels heavy or depressed, or if you are ill or distressed much of the time there, try to find out whether or not your feeling has any connection to underground sha, or noxious energy.

The first thing to do is tune in to the state of energy underground. Decide how to arrange your line of questioning. Make sure your questions are clear and simple. Write them down if you wish. Then relax for a minute or so before you begin the actual dowsing. Your first question should be: "Is there sha here?" If you receive a yes answer, you should ask if it is coming from below ground, from negative memory, or from something aboveground. You could ask if the sha is in the form of a noxious ray or a negative force field. You can then probe for its cause. It could be coming from an underground stream, a crossing of underground streams, an underground pool or well, a cave, sharp rock, or ridge pointing up from below ground, a fissure, a fault line, bad soil conditions, a buried tree stump, underground pollution.

If you find out that there is a noxious ray, you then have to find out where it enters your space. You can do this by dowsing on your floor plan. The easiest way to do it is to hold the pendulum with one hand while pointing with the index finger of the other hand to the outline of the floor plan. It doesn't matter where you start. Slowly move your pointing finger bit by bit around the outline and ask, "Does it enter here? Does it enter here?" until the pendulum gives you a clear yes.

The easiest cure for this fairly common problem of a noxious ray is to draw three concentric arcs in blue ink or blue pencil around the spot where the ray enters, as shown in figure 205. It works.

Another cure for noxious rays, which also works for negative force fields, is to take a copy of your floor plan and paste it on a board or stiff piece of cardboard that will not bend. Then take copper wire and tape it along the entire outline of the floor plan—but don't join the ends of the wire. They must not touch. Cut the wire a bit short. Once you've done this, put the floor plan away for safekeeping.

Another cure for a noxious ray, depending on the light, is to place a potted plant at the spot where the ray enters, as shown in figure 206, and then take copper wire and coil it up the outside of the pot in a spiral, making sure to attach it securely with tape.

(fig. 205)   *(fig. 206)*

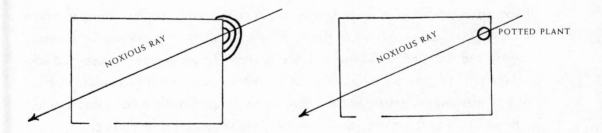

A cure that sometimes works for a place built over an underground stream is to put potted plants over the course of the stream. They will absorb and convert the water chi to make the place feel healthier.

If you live in the countryside and find underground sha connected to a line of electromagnetic energy, you can trace it to the point where the negative energy emanates, or at least to a point where it can be treated. It may be a point where two lines cross. Once you have it precisely located, you can transform the chi by driving an iron or steel rod or pipe, about three feet long, into the ground; by planting several trees around the point; by forming a circle of heavy rocks around the point; or by forming a spiral around the point with rocks, beginning on the point and moving counterclockwise.

The method for map dowsing for underground streams and lines of energy is similar to the method used for finding noxious rays. The only difference is that you have to explore the entire area, not just the outline. The easiest way to do this is to first draw a grid over your floor plan or property map. The finer the grid, the more precise your findings will be. Pointing to each of the squares in sequence ask, "Is it here? Is it here?" A pattern will show up.

A cure I have used for high-frequency rays coming through a wall is to find the point of entry and place a large crock filled with stones there.

No matter what material you use for your cure, always dowse over it first to find out whether it is appropriate or not.

The correct approach to divining can be summed up in three steps: getting your question clear, tuning in on the object of your search, and allowing your intuition to guide you.

SPACE PURIFICATION: HEALING NEGATIVE MEMORY

If you discover that your space holds a negative memory, you can dowse to find out what it is. Cities are full of them. They are caused by every sort of human tragedy and suffering, including violence, divorce, financial ruin, disease, and so on, and on a larger scale by burial grounds, battlefields, an old execution ground such as Washington Square in New York, or an old prison site such as the Bastille in Paris. The way to clear negative memory involves purification practice.

The environment, in a very profound sense, is the collective mental projection of countless sentient beings. Therefore, actions to purify and bless it must be done completely selflessly and compassionately.

The following practice is an excellent technique for environmental purification. It should be done with pure intentions, with perfect detachment, and with loving-kindness and compassion. It is called "Sending and Receiving." It is best to sit in a meditation posture, although you can stand, walk, or lie down.

Breathe in and fill your heart center with all the negative memory, all the suffering you perceive in the environment. Visualize it turning blue-black in your heart center. Then, as your breath turns, transform the negative energy, or blue-black light to diamond-white light. Breathe this diamond-white light out and fill the environment with it. Your breathing does not have to be deep. It should be natural and easy. Don't strain. The power of your concentration is what is important here.

The amount of time it takes to do this practice depends entirely on your intuitive sense. When you feel complete with your practice, simply release it, and dedicate your practice to the joy and contentment of all sentient beings in the universe.

AFTERWORD

In my ten years of practice I have seen over and over again how my clients, who focus on their home and environment and make changes according to the principles of feng shui, change their lives for the better.

The ancient Taoist arts, of which feng shui is an integral part, have roots that reach far beyond Chinese history and culture to a world of which little is known. Yet practicing the timeless principles of these arts can enable us to live in harmony with the rhythms of the universe and receive the blessings of long life, happiness, and abundance.

The condition of our environment depends ultimately upon how we relate to one another. Healthy and pleasant environmental conditions naturally arise when we cultivate pure awareness and equanimity in ourselves while practicing kindness and compassion toward others.

I wish you luck in using this book. If you want help, or have ideas or experiences with feng shui you wish to share, you can write to me at the following address: T. Raphael Simons, 545 8th Avenue, Suite 401, New York, NY 10018.

APPENDICES

THE FIVE ELEMENTS

ELEMENT	SEASON	SHAPE	COLORS	DIRECTIONS IN SPACE
Water	winter	undulant asymmetrical	black, navy	north
Wood	spring	rectangular	green, light blue	east, southeast
Fire	summer	triangular	red, purple	south
Earth	late summer	square, flat	yellow	southwest, middle, northeast
Metal	autumn	round, oval	white	west, northwest

The Eight Points

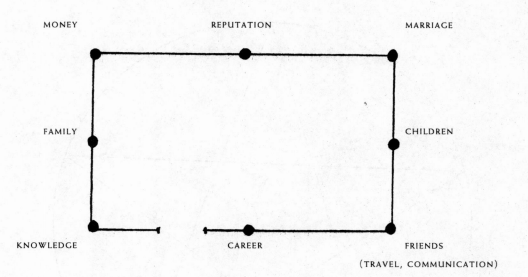

MONEY   REPUTATION   MARRIAGE

FAMILY   CHILDREN

KNOWLEDGE   CAREER   FRIENDS
                                              (TRAVEL, COMMUNICATION)

THE THREE CYCLES

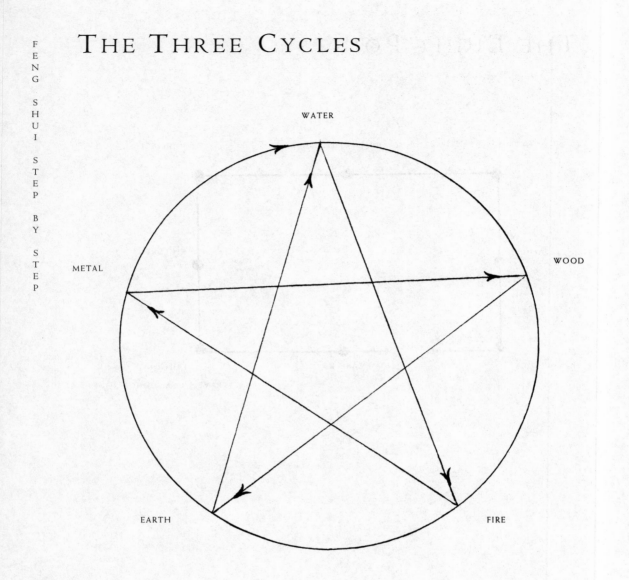

THE CYCLE OF GENERATION

Water generates Wood
Wood generates Fire
Fire generates Earth
Earth generates Metal
Metal generates Water

THE CYCLE OF DESTRUCTION

Water destroys Fire
Fire destroys Metal
Metal destroys Wood
Wood destroys Earth
Earth destroys Water

THE CYCLE OF MITIGATION

Water mitigates the conflict of Metal with Wood
Wood mitigates the conflict of Water with Fire
Fire mitigates the conflict of Wood with Earth
Earth mitigates the conflict of Fire with Metal
Metal mitigates the conflict of Earth with Water

The Nine Birth Stars

Star	Color	Principal Direction in Space	Harmonious Directions in Space
1 Water	black, navy	north	west, northwest, east, southeast
2 Earth	yellow	southwest	west, northwest, northeast, south
3 Wood	green, light blue	east	north, southeast, south
4 Wood	green, light blue	southeast	north, east, south
5 Earth	yellow	middle	southwest, west, northwest, northeast, south
6 Metal	white	northwest	southwest, west, north, northeast
7 Metal	white	west	southwest, northwest, north, northeast
8 Earth	yellow	northeast	southwest, west, northwest, south
9 Fire	red, purple	south	east, southeast, southwest, northeast

THE LUCKY STARS

STAR	COLOR	DIRECTION IN SPACE
1 Water	white	north
2 Earth	black	southwest
3 Wood	jade green	east
4 Wood	green	southeast
5 Earth	yellow	middle
6 Metal	white	northwest
7 Metal	red	west
8 Earth	white	northeast
9 Fire	purple	south

INDEX

ABOUT THE AUTHOR

T. Raphael Simons, who holds degrees in piano and musical composition and taught at Princeton and Oberlin before turning to occult science, began his apprenticeship in feng shui and astrology with Chinese Master Terry Lee in New York in 1986. Simons's ability to read Chinese has enabled him to understand authentic methods in a way that few Westerners have been privileged to do, and his knowledge of both astrology and feng shui give his interpretations an added depth. He also studied Western astrology with the late Ivy M. G. Jacobson and served as one of her teaching assistants. Mr. Simons now holds private consultations in the New York area and in Arizona and frequently lectures at the Learning Annex in New York.